GOSPEL
F⊕UNDATIONS

THE GOD WHO CREATES
VOL. 1 | Genesis

1

From the creators of *The Gospel Project*, *Gospel Foundations* is a six-volume resource that teaches the storyline of Scripture. It is comprehensive in scope yet concise enough to be completed in just one year. Each seven-session volume includes videos to help your group understand the way each text fits into the storyline of the Bible.

© 2018 Lifeway Press®

Reprinted Oct. 2018, Sept. 2020, Mar. 2021

ISBN 9781462798087 • Item 005802699

Dewey decimal classification: 230

Subject headings: CHRISTIANITY / GOSPEL / SALVATION

EDITORIAL TEAM

Ben Trueblood
Director, Student Ministry

JohnPaul Basham
Manager, Student Ministry Publishing

Andy McLean
Content Editor

Grace Pepper
Production Editor

Alli Quattlebaum
Graphic Designer

We believe that the Bible has God for its author; salvation for its end; and truth, without any mixture of error, for its matter and that all Scripture is totally true and trustworthy. To review Lifeway's doctrinal guideline, please visit lifeway.com/doctrinalguideline.

To order additional copies of this resource, write to Lifeway Resources Customer Service; One Lifeway Plaza; Nashville, TN 37234; fax 615-251-5933; call toll free 800-458-2772; order online at Lifeway.com; email orderentry@lifeway.com; or visit the Lifeway Christian Store serving you.

Printed in the United States of America

Student Ministry Publishing
Lifeway Resources
One Lifeway Plaza
Nashville, TN 37234

CONTENTS

ABOUT *THE GOSPEL PROJECT*

Gospel Foundations is from the creators of *The Gospel Project*, which exists to point kids, students, and adults to the gospel of Jesus Christ through weekly group Bible studies and additional resources that show how God's plan of redemption unfolds throughout Scripture and still today, compelling them to join the mission of God.

The Gospel Project provides theological yet practical, age-appropriate Bible studies that immerse your entire church in the story of the gospel, helping to develop a gospel culture that leads to gospel mission:

Gospel Story
Immersing people of all ages in the storyline of Scripture: God's plan to rescue and redeem His creation through His Son, Jesus Christ.

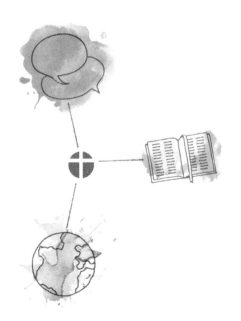

Gospel Culture
Inspiring communities where the gospel saturates our experience and doubters become believers who become declarers of the gospel.

Gospel Mission
Empowering believers to live on mission, declaring the good news of the gospel in word and deed.

HOW TO USE THIS STUDY

This Bible-study book includes seven weeks of content for group and personal study. Each session is divided into the following components:

Introduction

Every session contains an intro option for your group time, allowing there to be a natural transition into the material for that week.

Setting the Context

This section is designed to provide the context to the biblical passage being discussed. It will help group members to better understand the passage under consideration for each session, as well as how the biblical storyline connects between each session. It is also in this section that you will find the reference to the informational graphic for each session, once again helping students to develop a deeper understanding into the storyline of Scripture.

Session Videos

Each session has a corresponding video to help tell the Bible story. After watching the video, spend some time discussing the questions provided, as well as any additional questions raised by your students in response to the video.

Group Discussion

After watching the video, continue the group discussion by reading the Scripture passages and discussing the questions on these pages. Additional content is provided on these pages to grant further clarity into the meaning of these passages. Also, it is in this section that you find the Christ Connection, showing students how all of Scripture points to Jesus.

Head, Heart, Hands

This section is designed to close out your group time by personally reflecting on how God's Story challenges the way we think, feel, and live as a result. Because God's Word is capable of changing everything about a person, this section seeks to spell out how each session is able to transform our Heads, Hearts, and Hands.

Personal Study

Five personal devotions are provided for each session to take individuals deeper into Scripture and to supplement the content introduced in the group study. With biblical teaching and introspective questions, these sections challenge individuals to grow in their understanding of God's Word and to respond in faith.

GOD'S WORD TO YOU

A SUMMARY OF THE BIBLE

In the beginning, the all-powerful, personal God created the universe. This God created human beings in His image to live joyfully in His presence, in humble submission to His gracious authority. But all of us have rebelled against God and, in consequence, must suffer the punishment of our rebellion: physical death and the wrath of God.

Thankfully, God initiated a rescue plan, which began with His choosing the nation of Israel to display His glory in a fallen world. The Bible describes how God acted mightily on Israel's behalf, rescuing His people from slavery and then giving them His holy law. But God's people—like all of us—failed to rightly reflect the glory of God.

Then, in the fullness of time, in the person of Jesus Christ, God Himself came to renew the world and to restore His people. Jesus perfectly obeyed the law given to Israel. Though innocent, He suffered the consequences of human rebellion by His death on a cross. But three days later, God raised Him from the dead.

Now the church of Jesus Christ has been commissioned by God to take the news of Christ's work to the world. Empowered by God's Spirit, the church calls all people everywhere to repent of sin and to trust in Christ alone for our forgiveness. Repentance and faith restores our relationship with God and results in a life of ongoing transformation.

The Bible promises that Jesus Christ will return to this earth as the conquering King. Only those who live in repentant faith in Christ will escape God's judgment and live joyfully in God's presence for all eternity. God's message is the same to all of us: repent and believe, before it is too late. Confess with your mouth that Jesus is Lord and believe with your heart that God raised Him from the dead, and you will be saved.

GOD CREATES

*IN THE BEGINNING, GOD CREATED EVERYTHING,
AND HE CREATED EVERYTHING GOOD.*

INTRODUCTION

Every story has a beginning. The story of the Bible begins with four astounding words: "In the beginning God…" (Gen. 1:1). Often, people are tempted to take God's presence in the beginning for granted and fail to recognize the power it implies. In fact, God wasn't just there at the beginning; He was there before the beginning.

Every physical thing in the universe has an origin. That's as true of you and me as it is of the most magnificent stars in the farthest galaxies. Everything that exists once did not. If you were to travel back in time, you would reach a point when everything and everyone in existence fades into nothingness.

Everything and everyone, that is, except God. Before the first four words of Genesis 1, before the stars filled the night sky, before God breathed life into the dust and made man, God alone was there. "In the beginning God…" (Gen. 1:1) is really just another way of saying, "Before the beginning, God was there."

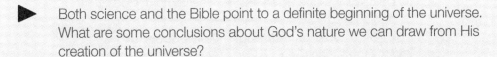 Both science and the Bible point to a definite beginning of the universe. What are some conclusions about God's nature we can draw from His creation of the universe?

SETTING THE CONTEXT

God was there at the beginning of the story line of Scripture—and so was the Son of God, which the New Testament makes explicit: The Son is before all things and He created all things (Col. 1:16-17). "Seeing Jesus in Genesis" (p. 10) shows just some of the ways the centrality of Jesus in Scripture was the plan of God from the very beginning.

Also vital to the beginning of Scripture is the doctrine of creation *ex nihilo*, a Latin phrase that means "out of nothing." We use the word create when we cause something to come into being, but we always form something out of other things that previously existed. We create music using notes, art out of paints and a canvas, books from words, language, paper, and binding.

God, however, created from nothing. Everything in existence came to be because of Him—rocks, trees, the very air we breathe. Not only that, but non-tangible realities such as courage, love, and laughter came from Him as well. All of this came from the heart of God at the beginning.

SEEING
JESUS *IN* GENESIS

OLD TESTAMENT	*NEW TESTAMENT*
The First Adam Brought Death (Gen. 3)	**The Second Adam** Brought Life (Rom. 5)
The Protoevangelium The Promise of Deliverance from the Serpent (Gen. 3:15)	**The Fulfillment** Jesus Destroys the Works of the Devil (1 John 3:8)
Abel's Blood Cries Out for Justice (Gen. 4)	**Jesus' Blood** Proclaims Forgiveness (Heb. 12:24)
The Almost Sacrifice of Isaac "The LORD Will Provide" (Gen. 22)	**The Crucifixion of Jesus** "The Lamb of God" (John 1:29)
Joseph Suffered According to God's Plan (Gen. 50:20)	**Jesus Suffered** According to God's Plan (Acts 2:23)

SESSION VIDEOS

Watch this session's video, and then continue the group discussion using the following guide.

▶ What ideas or phrases stood out to you most in the video? Why?

▶ In what ways is the biblical truth that human beings are the pinnacle of God's creation affirmed in our culture? Denied in our culture?

GROUP DISCUSSION

As a group, read Genesis 1:1-2,31.

⭐ What are some of the things we can learn about the nature and character of God from these verses alone?

⭐ Why does God call each step of His creation good?

▶ Is it morally good? How so?
Is it aesthetically good? How so?
Is it usable? How so?

While these things are certainly good, the ultimate purpose and design of creation is to declare God's glory and proclaim the work of His hands (Ps. 19:1) and to reveal things about God that are invisible to us, such as His eternal power and divine nature (Rom. 1:20). Because of creation, we can clearly see and understand these things.

As a group, read Genesis 1:26-28; 2:16-25.

▶ What is different about the way God created humans from everything else?

▶ What do you think it means to be created in God's image?

⭐ Why is it important that we recognize that all humans are created in God's image?

To bear God's image means:

1 To have a relationship with Him.

Our image-bearing started when God created us. The account in Genesis shows how powerful a scene this was—when God's face was toward us, when He breathed into the first man the breath of life. Just as a mirror best reflects an image when the mirror is directly in front of the object, we reflect God's image best when we are in close relationship with Him.

To be created in God's image means that we have a unique ability to relate intimately with God and others. When we recognize this fact, we can only conclude that every human being is deserving of respect and honor.

▶ In what ways can your life demonstrate the priority of your relationship with God?

2 To bear God's image doesn't point only to the relationship we have with God; we also have a relationship with one another. God created us "male and female." The God who exists in community—Father, Son, and Holy Spirit—created human beings to live in community as well.

In fact, verses 22-24 tell us that we were not created to bear God's image on our own or to have an isolated relationship with God. We reflect God best when we are in community with one another—relating to others in love and grace. Thus, reflecting God's image means we are to relate rightly to Him and to others.

▶ How are Jesus' remarks in John 13:35 a reflection of people living out the image of God in their relationships with others?

3 Reflecting God also goes beyond our relationships and is seen in the rhythms of our everyday activities and rest.

A lot of people have wrongly assumed that the command to work was a result of man's sinning and rebelling against God. But the creation narrative shows us that God created work for man as part of His good world. Work is just as beautiful as the sunset, and just as purposeful as the rain.

Work isn't something that God gave man as a curse after the fall into sin; the toil of work is what came with sin, but work itself is designed to give us fulfillment and provide us an environment to reflect God. When viewed rightly, our work can reflect God. But not only does our work reflect God, our resting does as well. In fact, God commands us to rest.

▶ How can you reflect God in your work as a student? an athlete? in a part-time job?

As a group, read Colossians 1:15-17.

▶ What description of Jesus sticks out to you the most in these verses?

▶ What do these verses tell us about the process and purpose of creation?

★ How does it change our overall perspective to recognize that all things were created by the Son and for the Son?

The Bible is a God-centered book. We have been given Scripture so that we might know God. That means when we read Scripture, we should focus primarily on what we can learn, love, and embrace about God and His Son, Jesus.

CHRIST CONNECTION

Jesus is the perfect image of the invisible God, the only One who rules wisely over creation, perfectly relates to God and others, and through His work, earns our everlasting rest. By the Son, for the Son, and through the Son, all things exist and hold together.

OUR MISSION

◯ Head

How does knowledge of God's sovereignty over all creation influence the way you think about your circumstances?

How should the doctrine of humans being created in God's image influence the way we think about others?

♥ Heart

How should the doctrine of humans being created in God's image influence the way we feel about others, both Christians and non-Christians?

Why should we be grieved when we see image-bearers of God living in a way that is contrary to the way God intended?

✋ Hands

How will you begin to treat friends, family members, and even strangers differently based upon the truth that they are created in God's image?

What are some ways you can begin to reflect God by being a better steward of the world He has given us?

PERSONAL STUDY: DAY 1

✪ The point: God created everything.

▶ **Read Genesis 1:1.**

In verse 1, the Bible introduces the concept of the heavens and the earth. What Person is also introduced here? How is this significant? Explain.

What was the action that occurred in verse 1? Why do you think it's important to realize that God was the one to take this action?

How does verse 1 go against what so much of our culture believes? Why is it important for believers to understand this foundational truth?

Underline the words God used to describe the earth in verse 2.

The word *create* means to bring into existence. God created everything from nothing, but even more amazing is the truth that God already was, before anything else existed. The fact that God created everything means that nothing, other than God Himself, is eternal.

While many in our culture believe that the universe sprang into existence from nothing, such beliefs are implausible, and science itself testifies to this. According to the standard scientific beliefs in cosmology, the finite universe came into existence at a certain point in time/space/history. Since both science and philosophy discredit the claim that something can come from nothing, the empirical knowledge we have makes it look more and more like the Christian worldview gets it right on the creation account.

How does knowing that we have a Creator change the way believers view our meaning and purpose?

▶ **Respond**

Journal your thoughts on this: *The God who existed before the world began is the same God who made me.*

Jot down a few ways you can look at life differently, knowing that the eternal God created you, loves you, and wants a relationship with you.

15

⭐ The point: God created everything good.

What comes to mind when you hear the word *good*? A good person? A good movie? A good day? A good game? Considering all of these phrases, what is your personal definition of the word *good*?

▶ **Read Genesis 1:3-25.**

Briefly describe what God created on each day.

First Day:

Fourth Day:

Second Day:

Fifth Day:

Third Day:

At the end of each day, God was pleased with what He had made. Circle each instance of "God saw that it was good."

Why is it important that God saw creation as good? What are the implications for our lives now?

God's definition of *good* is sometimes different than our own. God's creation was good because it fulfilled its main purpose: to display His glory. Everything beautiful tells of His beauty. Everything He made is good because He is good.

▶ **Respond**

If the weather permits, go outside and take a short walk. Spend a few minutes listening, looking around, and paying attention to the smell. Notice the parts of God's creation you usually pass by.

PERSONAL STUDY: DAY 3

⭐ **The point: God created everything through His Son.**

▶ **Read John 1:1-3,14.**

As Christians, we believe in the *Trinity*—that *God is One, in three persons: God the Father, Jesus the Son*, and the *Holy Spirit* (See John 14). Combining this belief with what we read earlier this week, we know that in the beginning, all three persons of the Trinity were present: God, Jesus, and the Holy Spirit.

List the three things John said about "the Word" in verse 1.

Read through the verses once more, replacing "the Word" with Jesus. How does this help your understanding of these verses? Explain.

According to these verses, how was everything created? Why is this important?

Summarize the truth of verse 14 in your own words. What is so significant about the fact that Jesus took on flesh and walked on earth with His people?

▶ **Read Colossians 1:15-17.**

Jesus is the perfect image of the invisible God, the only One who rules wisely over creation, perfectly relates to God and others, and through His work, earns our everlasting rest. By the Son, for the Son, and through the Son, all things exist and hold together.

▶ **Respond**

How does understanding that the entire Bible is the story of Jesus change the way you approach reading it?

What are some areas of your life in which you need to remember that Jesus holds all things together?

⭐ **The point: We reflect God in how we rule wisely over the world.**

▶ **Read Genesis 1:26-31.**

Summarize verse 26 in your own words. How does knowing we are made in God's image and likeness affect the way we live and rule over His creation?

According to verse 27, both men and women were created _____ _____ _____ _____ _____. Why is this significant?

Using verses 28-30, list what God instructed Adam and Eve to rule over, as well as what He told them to use.

Rule

Use

God created everything, and He has ultimate power and control over everything. Still, He made us in His image, and then gave us authority to rule over creation.

What do you think this shows about God's character? Explain.

▶ **Respond**

Think about items, people, or tasks you have a responsibility to rule wisely over. What are some ways you can influence each area in a way that reflects God?

God created the world, which speaks of Him, and He created us, who bear His image. The way we interact with the world around us also speaks of Him. Ask the Holy Spirit to help you wisely influence the people, places, and things around you for God's glory.

PERSONAL STUDY: DAY 5

⭐ **The point: We reflect God in how we relate to Him and others.**

▶ **Read Genesis 2:4-9,16-25.**

Verses 4-7 summarize the creation of the heavens and the earth, as well as man. Before God created man to cultivate the earth, how did things survive?

God could have sustained the earth on His own, but He made Adam to take care of His creation. This was the beginning of the first relationship—between God and man.

Considering this, why do you think it's important that God "placed" man in the garden (v. 8)?

What are the implications of God's command in verses 16-17? Why are these commands significant?

The animals weren't enough to complement Adam and be His helper, so God created another human—woman. Community and relationships are important to God. From the beginning, God didn't intend for people to be alone.

Circle Adam's job in verses 19-20.

Although God gave Adam an important job to do, even that work couldn't fulfill him. He needed a helper, so God created Eve. God had established the second relationship, this time between man and woman.

What is unique about the way God created Eve from the way He created Adam or the rest of creation?

▶ **Respond**

The first relationship God created was between Himself and man, and the second was between man and woman. Our relationship with God should always come first. Does your life currently reflect this priority?

Do your current relationships bear the image God intended? What are some ways you are accomplishing God's work together with the people in your life?

MAN SINS

SIN CORRUPTS GOD'S GOOD CREATION.

INTRODUCTION

As a society, we don't seem to agree on much. Actually, about the only thing we might all agree on is that something is not right with the world. The broken world we see on the news, streaming through our social media feeds, or in the lives of our loved ones stresses one key truth: Somewhere at some time in our history, something went horribly, tragically wrong.

Most of us assume the problem is "out there" somewhere. Maybe you believe there are good people and bad people, and bad people cause all the trouble for good people. Or maybe you think the real problems are more systemic—poverty, lack of education, unequal opportunities, or the breakdown of the family structure.

What if the problem is not just out there, but in us? What if that outburst of anger you explained away wasn't just a result of stress, but reflected something you truly believed? What if that cutting remark wasn't just a slip of the tongue, but a hint at the real, unfiltered you? Maybe the problem is deeper than we know or care to admit.

 How would you define sin?

SETTING THE CONTEXT

God's creation was good. It was very good, in fact. The first man and woman lived together in God's garden where He had placed them, and they did the good work of representing His image in creation and living in a harmonious relationship with one another and God.

It's at this point in the story that we are introduced to another character, one that was not content with his place in creation. Here was a being that did not want to serve God as Creator but instead wanted to be God himself. Not only that, this creature desired that people—God's prized creation—adopt the same self-determining attitude and throw off the loving rule and reign of God. He would tempt the first humans to join him in his rebellion by inviting them to violate the single prohibition God had lovingly given them—not to eat from the one forbidden tree in the garden.

SALVATION *THROUGH JUDGMENT*

Judgment	The Event	The Means	Salvation
The Wicked	*The Flood* *Genesis 6:9*	*Floodwater*	**Noah and His Family**
The Egyptians	*The Exodus* *Exodus 1-15*	*The Plagues and the Red Sea*	**The Israelites**
Judah and Jerusalem	*The Exile* *2 Chron. 36*	*The Babylonians*	**The Remnant**
Sinners/ Jesus Christ	*The Cross* *Romans 5*	*God's Wrath and Our Substitute*	**Believers in Christ**
God's Enemies	*The Final Judgment* *2 Thess. 1*	*God's Wrath and Hell*	**God's People**

SESSION VIDEOS

Watch this session's video, and then continue the group discussion using the following guide.

▶ What ideas or phrases stood out to you most in the video? Why?

▶ What images or phrases about sin were most striking to you in the video? Why?

GROUP DISCUSSION

As a group, read Genesis 3:1-7.

 Look closely at the serpent's words. What was he implying about the nature and character of God through this temptation?

 What can we learn about our own sin from the serpent's temptation and Adam and Eve's response?

▶ What are some of the noticeable effects of sin you see in this passage?

As we begin to read the opening verses in chapter 3, we see that a drastic change is about to take place between humanity's relationship with their Creator. And at the heart of this change lies an issue of trust—trusting the goodness of God and His Word. In fact, distrust is at the heart of human rebellion. Human rebellion leads us to distrust the goodness of God's Word. This is at the heart of human sinfulness, so it's no surprise that Satan (disguised as a serpent) chose this line of temptation in the garden of Eden.

▶ When have you seen people disbelieve what God has clearly said?

As a group, read Genesis 6:5-7.

The text says God "was deeply grieved" over this entire situation. The Hebrew word used here means wounded, pained, or heartbroken. In Isaiah 54:6, the prophet used the same word to describe the feeling a wife would have if her husband abandoned her. Honestly, it's a strange word to use when talking about God because it makes Him sound incredibly vulnerable. God was not just angry over sin, but grieved and heartbroken by it. Sin is never primarily about breaking rules, but about wounding a relationship. When we sin, we betray our loving God and break His heart.

⭐ The Bible tells us that God grieved before His judgment took place. What does this tell us about His character and how He views sin in our lives?

Our instinctive response to the judgment of our sin is to wonder if God has gone too far. It doesn't seem befitting of a loving God to purge the earth like this. But consider what you might do if someone you love was being ravaged by cancer. You would take radical measures (like chemotherapy) to cleanse them from the cancer—not in spite of your love for them, but because of that love. That's precisely what God does with His creation. He loves it too much to let the cancer of our sin spread another inch.

▶ How would your attitude toward sin change if you saw it less as breaking God's rules and more as breaking God's heart?

▶ What are some things that might grieve God today? In what ways does He still show patience to His people?

God could have destroyed the world and all its inhabitants, but instead He chose to purge creation of its great wickedness. Yet, He would save one family. He chose not to give up on all humanity, not to turn His back and start over completely. Even though He knew Noah and his descendants would again disappoint Him, defy Him, and walk in faithlessness, God decided to preserve this remnant. Why? Because like a father who will not stop loving his children no matter how often they disobey, God bound His heart to His people.

Ultimately, sin became so great on earth that God decided to wipe creation clean with a worldwide flood. But in His grace, God made a way for His judgment of the wicked to lead to the salvation of Noah and his family. "Salvation Through Judgment" (p. 22) shows how this event foreshadows the cross of Jesus Christ and God's eternal plan of rescue for His people, for those who believe in His Son.

As a group, read Genesis 11:1-9.

At this point in the Genesis account is an interesting story, often called The Tower of Babel. Some time had passed since the judgment and mercy of the flood, but humanity was still broken from the inside out. There was still a sin problem because there was still a heart problem. Sin remained in people's hearts after the flood. God knew this was true—the flood was only meant to slow down the progression of sin in the world.

⭐ How did the people's work demonstrate a prideful disobedience?

God isn't against cities and towers, of course, but the architecture itself wasn't the issue that day; it was the motivation behind the city and tower. It was the wayward heart of humanity. The people wanted to build a city with a tower so high that they would make a name for themselves. Feel the arrogance of this statement. They stood in direct contrast to God's promise to give Abram a great name in Genesis 12. But these people wanted to achieve greatness for themselves. Notice in the last line of verse 4 that they were acting directly against God's good command to fill the earth by wanting to huddle together and build their own kingdom.

▶ In what ways might people in today's culture try to make a name for themselves?

▶ How might pursuing a bigger platform or a personal brand be the equivalent of trying to build our own kingdom?

CHRIST CONNECTION

Our sin reveals the depth of our rebellion against God and our helplessness to do anything to be right with God again. But what we cannot do, God has done through Jesus. Jesus is the Son of Eve whom God graciously provided to crush the head of the serpent Satan and rescue us from sin and death. (Genesis 3:15)

OUR MISSION

Head

How has this session altered your perception of sin?

How might a right perspective on sin help us have a right understanding of God's grace?

Heart

What happens when you only focus only on the behavioral aspect of sin and not on what is taking place within the heart?

How does the truth that God is grieved by our sin influence the way you deal with personal sin and temptation?

Hands

How can you trust in God's Word this week? How might that affect different areas of your life?

What opportunities has God given me in my neighborhood, school, community, and beyond to make God's name great and proclaim His kingdom?

⭐ **The point: Human rebellion leads us to distrust the goodness of God's Word.**

Has anyone ever told you a lie about someone? How did the lie affect your view of both people?

Lies affect our outlook on different situations and people. Adam and Eve trusted the serpent's lies rather than God.

▶ **Read Genesis 3:1-7.**

By trusting what the serpent said about God, Adam and Eve questioned God's goodness. How did the serpent create doubt about God's command?

▶ **Read Genesis 2:15-17.**

How did the serpent twist God's words? What did God actually say to Adam and Eve?

God's Words	The Serpent's Twist

What did Eve add to God's original commands?

People often forget that sin is actually rebellion against God (Isa. 1:2). Because the core of human rebellion involves mistrusting what God said, Satan's introduction of this doubt was critical. He attempts to do the same to believers today, tempting us to give in to sin.

▶ **Respond**

Consider this: *Are there areas in my own life where I'm tempted to doubt God's goodness?* Jot down a few areas and ask, "how your life might look different if you trusted in God's goodness in each of those areas."

PERSONAL STUDY: DAY 2

⭐ **The point: Human rebellion ruptures our relationship with God and others.**

▶ **Read Genesis 3:8-16.**

Humanity's rebellion against God resulted in our relationships with God and each other being broken. List Adam and Eve's actions in verses 8-10 that reveal a broken relationship with God.

Notice Adam heard God "in the garden" (v. 10). What does this reveal about the closeness of God's relationship with Adam and Eve?

According to verse 10, why did Adam and Eve hide from God?

Verse 11 demonstrates that Adam and Eve didn't previously have knowledge of their nakedness. What did God's second question imply?

Where did Adam shift the blame for his sin? Where did Eve shift the blame for her sin? In what ways do people often react this way today?

Make a note of God's punishment to both the serpent and the woman.

The Serpent	The Woman

▶ **Respond**

Prayerfully consider any broken relationships that might be present in your own life. Then, take a moment to jot down the names of those people. Pray for that relationship and the individual/group involved. Ask forgiveness from the individual/group.
Offer forgiveness to the individual/group.

PERSONAL STUDY: DAY 3

⭐ The point: God judges wickedness.

Grief may be technically defined as experiencing extreme mental pain due to loss or sorrow. What is another way you might describe grief in your own words.

▶ **Read Genesis 6:5-7.**

Reread verses 5-6 and fill in the blanks.

God saw that man's wickedness was _____.
Man's mind was on nothing but _____.
The Lord regretted He _____ _____ _____.

According to verse 6, what did God experience in response to widespread sin?

What was God's reaction to His people turning their hearts over to evil?

Judgment is God's response to sin. He is holy and righteous, and He will not continue to tolerate willful sin in His creation. God's decision to destroy parts of His creation was His judgment for sin at the time of the flood.

Name a few other places in the Bible where God was grieved by His people's sin, yet patient in His judgment.

▶ **Respond**

God created us for His glory (Isa. 43:7). Any time we choose not to live according to His glory, we sin (Rom. 3:23). Just like mankind at the time of Genesis 6, we are sinful and often choose disobedience.

God is grieved by sin (Ps. 78:40; Isa. 63:10). It causes Him agony and pain. Ask the Holy Spirit to guide you as you examine your heart. Confess to the Lord any sin in your life, repenting for any grief you have caused Him.

What is one sin that interferes with you focusing your mind and heart on God? If nothing in particular immediately comes to mind, ask God to reveal that sin to you today.

⭐ **The point: God provides a way of escape.**

▶ **Read Genesis 6:8-22.**

List the four ways Noah was described in verses 8-9.

Jot down the two words used to explain the state of the world in verse 11.

Underline the word "every" each time it appears in verses 12 and 13. What was God's plan for the inhabitants of the earth?

Briefly describe the scene depicted in verses 14-16.

How did God physically provide a way of escape for the righteous in this passage?

God told Noah He would destroy the earth with a _____. Who would be saved from the flood?

Noah received favor from God (Gen. 6:8). God's favor is His special blessing or approval. In response, Noah chose to live righteously and blamelessly (Gen. 6:9). Because of Noah's righteousness, his entire family would be saved from the flood.

In light of this, why do you think Noah's response was so important (v. 22)?

▶ **Respond**

This is so much more than the story of one man being saved from destruction; it begins the ongoing story of God using one man's righteousness to save humanity—Jesus.

We are not saved by our works, but by Jesus' righteousness. Thank God for providing a way for you to be saved.

⭐ **The point: God judges our attempts to build our own kingdom.**

The people of Shinar thought they could build a tower to reach into the heavens and make a name for themselves. However, God had a different plan.

▶ **Read Genesis 11:6-7.**

What made it easy for the people to work together to build the tower? Explain.

According to verse 6, what would happen if the men succeeded?

Why do you think God considered their "success" to be a negative thing? Explain.

What action did God take to respond to this situation?

God made men in His image and commissioned them to know and live according to His covenant. God knew that the men in Shinar were moving further away from His plan and His purpose. God didn't destroy the men; however, He destroyed their ability to carry out a plan that would cause them to lose sight of their need for Him.

▶ **Respond**

Sometimes you have a great plan and wonder why it falls apart. When you find yourself in this situation, stop and ask: *How often do I talk to God? How often do I hear from God? Was this my plan or God's plan?*

On a note card, write out these phrases:
• *God sees me.*
• *God cares for me.*
• *God knows any sin in my heart and will take steps to bring me back to Him.*

GOD MAKES A
COVENANT WITH ABRAHAM

*GOD CHOOSES A NATION TO REVERSE
THE CURSE OF SIN.*

INTRODUCTION

Trends show that people wait longer to get married and that fewer people get married today than in times past. But even though culture is changing, Americans are still fascinated with marriage, and for good reason. Marriage is a covenant relationship where a man and a woman make promises that bind them to each other for the rest of their lives. A covenant is an arrangement where both parties agree to keep their commitments no matter what.

Unfortunately, many people now approach marriage not so much as a covenant but more as a contract. In a contract, if one party breaks their side of the deal, then the contract becomes null and void—"I'll hold up my end of the bargain if you hold up your end."

This new reality changes our view not just of marriage, but also of our relationship with God. Why? Because the Bible describes God's relationship with His people as a covenant. Yet people often think of their relationship with God as a contract: "I have to do my part and be a good person, and if I do, then God will uphold His end of the deal by blessing me right now and taking me to heaven when I die."

 Consider your closest relationships. Are these relationships built on conditions? If so, how might that cause problems down the road?

SETTING THE CONTEXT

Genesis 3–11 is a downward spiral of humankind's sin where we see the devastating and far-reaching effects of the rebellion that began in Eden. Because of sin, every human relationship was broken—both with God and with each other.

Thanks to the genealogy listed in the second half of Genesis 11, we know that some three hundred years separate the tower of Babel and the beginning of Genesis 12. As Genesis 11 comes to an end, we are introduced to another character in the unfolding drama of Scripture—Abram. Very little is known about Abram's early life. He and his wife, Sarai, were childless (Gen. 11:30). He may have been a shepherd, and he was from the city of Ur (vv. 28,31). But God called this obscure man to be a pivotal piece in His plan of redemption, the first piece in reversing the curse of Babylon, for God planned to bless him and his descendants in a unique way. "Abram's Journey" (p. 34) shows the location of Ur and Abram's journey to a new land, which involved passing by and leaving behind Babylon.

Abram's *JOURNEY*

SESSION VIDEOS

Watch this session's video, and then continue the group discussion using the following guide.

▶ What ideas or phrases stood out to you most in the video? Why?

▶ What aspect of Abram's life and faith stuck out the most from the video? Why?

GROUP DISCUSSION

As we start with this story, we see from the very beginning that God has not given up on humanity. He still has a rescue plan in place, and that plan involves entering into a unique relationship with Abram.

As a group, read Genesis 12:1-4.

▶ Circle the uses of the pronoun *I* as it appears in God's words to Abram. What do you think this tells us about God's commitment to His glory and His plan of redemption?

Through Abram's descendants, God will reverse the misfortunes of Eden (separation from God) and Babel (separation from one another). The specific promises that God made to Abram make this connection with the events of Babel clear: the people of Babel wanted to "make a name" for themselves (Gen. 11:4), but God promised to make Abram's name great (12:2). The rebels at Babel were scattered over the earth under God's judgment, but through Abram God promised to bless "all the peoples on earth" (12:3).

▶ If you were Abram, how do you think you would have responded to such a call from God? What might have been some of your hesitations or objections?

⭐ What does Abram's response reveal about his faith and about the nature of faith in general?

God called Abram to leave all he knew and go to a new place God would eventually reveal to him. Abram demonstrated faith by responding positively, though he didn't know the specifics of God's call. God's plan was to make a covenant with Abram and use him as a vessel through whom He would bless all the nations of the earth.

As a group, read Genesis 15:1-6.

▶ Why was Abram struggling with the promises of God in these verses?

Sometimes evidence seems to stack up against promises. God made wonderful promises to Abram, but Abram and Sarai still didn't have any children. Both of them were old, and Sarai was well past the years of being able to conceive. So Abram began to question God's promise, and even took matters into his own hands.

⭐ What are some ways that we, like Abram, try to take matters into our own hands?

▶ How have you tried to "help" God? How did it turn out?

Often, we mistake God's apparent "inactivity" for "inability." We think God is not working at all just because He is not working how or when we would like or expect. This often leads us to either anxiety or outright rejection as we try to take matters into our own hands.

▶ Which one of these are you more inclined to: anxiety or rejection?

▶ How do both responses result from a failure to trust in the future promises of God?

God reassured Abram that he would have children of his own. He would give him offspring as numerous as the stars in the sky. Not only did God state this promise to Abram and his children repeatedly (see Gen. 22:17; 26:4; 28:14), but He saw it through. In Deuteronomy 1:10, Moses said, "The LORD your God has so multiplied you that today you are as numerous as the stars of the sky," and again in Deuteronomy 10:22: "Your fathers went down to Egypt, 70 people in all, and now the LORD your God has made you as numerous as the stars of the sky."

As a group, read Genesis 17:1-10.

▶ When have you felt like Abram, needing to be reminded of God's promises?

⭐ How did God set apart Abram and his offspring in this passage?

▶ In what ways does God call Christians to be set apart today?

Here we see how Abram's faith faltered somewhat as he and Sarai grew older and still did not have a child. God came to him again to reiterate the promises and His covenant commitment. This time He gave Abram a new name, and He gave him a sign of their covenant relationship—a sign that would set His people apart from the rest of the world. The Lord changed Abram's name to "Abraham," which means "father of a multitude" (17:5). Not only that, but God also changed Sarai's name to Sarah, which means "princess," because kings would come from Abraham's family. He would produce a royal line (leading, of course, to the King of kings—Jesus of Nazareth).

CHRIST CONNECTION

God promised Abraham that He would bless the world through his descendants. Jesus Christ is the promised descendant of Abraham through whom salvation flows to the world.

OUR MISSION

Head

God uses flawed and imperfect people in His good work in the world. What are some ways this encourages us?

William Carey once said, "Expect great things from God; attempt great things for God!" Where can you imagine yourself attempting great things for God as He continues to transform you more into the image of His Son?

Heart

How does knowing that God seeks after you encourage you to trust in Him?

How should knowing that God is the One who makes us righteous before Him motivate us to pursue lives of holiness?

Hands

What circumstances in your life tempt you to respond like Abraham did?

What are some ways you can live out a renewed faith this week, knowing God is in your corner and is working according to His perfect timetable?

PERSONAL STUDY: DAY 1

⭐ **The point: God initiates a renewed relationship.**

▶ **Read Genesis 12:1-4.**

Summarize God's command to Abram in verse 1.

What promises did God make to Abram?

Circle each occurrence of the pronoun *I*. Underline each occurrence of the pronouns *you* or *your*.

Look again at God's use of the pronouns *I*, *you*, and *your*. Who was responsible for and committed to fulfilling these promises? What was Abram's responsibility in seeing God fulfill these promises?

How did Abram respond to God's command? Explain.

How do God's promises to Abram connect back to the events of Babel?

▶ **Respond**

Recall times when you felt insignificant or unworthy. Journal about how God's promises to Abram encourage you. Then, list the ways God's promises to Abram are extended to you.

Ask God to help you fully obey Him, no matter what or where He calls you to.

For further study about relationship with God, read John 6:44; Romans 5:8; and 1 John 4:19.

⭐ **The point: God watches over Abram.**

▶ **Read Genesis 13-14.**

Why did Abram and Lot go separate paths?

Why do you think Abram went to try and rescue Lot?

Who is Melchizedek? Can you find him anywhere else in the Bible? What does it say about him there? (hint: check Book of Hebrews)

What did Melchizedek say about Abram?

Why wouldn't Abram take anything from the king of Sodom? Why is this important?

The story of Abram and Melchizedek at the end of Genesis 14 is confusing. Melchizedek seems to come out of nowhere and is referred to as the king of Salem and a priest of God. But after this brief encounter where he blessed Abram and Abram gave him a tenth of everything, this important man disappeared from the pages of Genesis. So who was Melchizedek?

Many believe Melchizedek was a theophany—an appearance of God in human form. Whether Melchizedek was indeed a theophany or just a mysterious man sent by God, we cannot miss God's heart for Abram in this moment. God reached out to Abram in his moment of victory to encourage him and remind him who truly delivered his enemies—it was God Most High.

▶ **Respond**

God was obviously watching over Abram during this rescue mission with Lot. Looking back, how can you point to God's protection over you in certain areas of your life?

PERSONAL STUDY: DAY 3

⭐ **The point: God commands us to trust His promises.**

▶ **Read Genesis 15:1-6.**

This passage starts out with a vision and a promise. In your own words, describe the vision God gave to Abram.

How would you expect God to respond to Abram as he struggled to believe? How did God respond?

Expected Response	God's Response

Why do you think God gave Abram the sign of the stars as a reminder of His promise?

▶ **Read Galatians 3:7.**

Summarize the truth of this Scripture. What does this mean for believers today?

What did God do in response to Abram's belief?

▶ **Respond**

List any of God's promises you've doubted recently. Ask God to strengthen your faith.

For further study on how God bound Himself to keep these promises to Abram, read Genesis 15:7-21.

⭐ **The point: God is able to fulfill His promises despite our mistakes.**

▶ **Read Genesis 16.**

Why do you think Sarai suggested that Abram have a child with her slave, Hagar?

Sarai thought she would help God's promises to come true even though she and Abram weren't having any children. When have you have tried to formulate a plan instead of just waiting and relying on God to come through?

How did Sarai respond when Hagar became pregnant? How did Abram respond?

How does this account depart from God's original design for marriage to be between one woman and one man?

How did God respond to Hagar? What does this say about His character?

When Hagar became pregnant, Sarai became bitterly jealous, eventually leading to Hagar and Ishmael being sent away (Gen. 21:8-21). But Abram and Sarai's act of doubt and disobedience did not end there. The descendants of Ishmael would plague the Israelites long after that time (Gen. 16:12).

Abram and Sarah failed to consider that their actions might have enduring consequences, which would affect many others. The same is true of us. We need to carefully consider whom we might bless by our obedience and whom we might hurt by our disobedience.

▶ **Respond**

What are some of your actions that have resulted in negative consequences? Pray and ask God for wisdom to make biblical and God-honoring decisions each day.

PERSONAL STUDY: DAY 5

⭐ **The point: God desires for His people to be set apart for His glory.**

▶ **Read Genesis 17:1-14.**

What was God's first command to Abram (v. 1)?

Twenty-four years had passed since God called Abram and promised to bless him (Gen. 12:4). How did Abram respond after the wait (v. 3)?

In verse 5, what new way did God affirm His promise to Abram?

Note what God promised Abram and what God required from him.

Promised	Required

How do you think God wants believers to be set apart today?

▶ **Respond**

Pray a prayer of thanks to God for His promises and ask Him to help you be a covenant-keeper.

For further study on what it means to be set apart, read Romans 12:1-2; 1 Corinthians 6:19; and 1 Peter 1:16; 2:9.

GOD TESTS ABRAHAM

FAITH IS TRUSTING IN THE PROMISES OF GOD.

INTRODUCTION

Think about what you love most in this world. Family. Reputation. Health. Possessions. Talents. Now, consider how you would respond if it were taken away from you. Someone you love dies. You lose your scholarship to college. Your home burns to the ground. What would your response be?

▶ How have you responded in times of loss, whether the losses were great or small?

Our response when what we love most is taken from us, or even when it appears that it could be taken from us, reveals much about our relationship with God. We know how we should respond, but how do we?

In these times of loss or potential loss, we have the opportunity to experience God deepening and refining our faith. It's not just a matter of submitting to God; God will do what He pleases! It's a matter of submitting willfully, faithfully, and joyfully. The pain of loss is very real—but the goodness of God is even more real. That is what must sustain us.

SETTING THE CONTEXT

Genesis 17 leaves Abraham with renewed confidence in God. During the long years of waiting for God to fulfill His promises to him, Abraham had wrestled with doubt. When would God provide an heir? Would He ever?

Abraham had another son, Ishmael, through Hagar, Sarah's maidservant (Gen. 16), but God's promise of offspring would come specifically through Sarah (17:19-22). And the Lord miraculously provided this "only son" of promise. "The Lord Will Provide" (p. 46) shows just a glimpse of the Lord's desire to provide for His people.

After years of waiting, Abraham and Sarah finally had a son, Isaac. God's long-promised blessing of descendants to Abraham was at last visibly being fulfilled, and Abraham was faithful to mark this son of the covenant in the way God had commanded him with circumcision.

We don't know how old Isaac was when Genesis 22 opens, but it's clear from his interactions with his father that a number of years had gone by. The treasured little boy had grown, and God was about to introduce the greatest test of Abraham's faith.

THE LORD *WILL PROVIDE*

	SUBJECT TO DEATH	*THE SUBSTITUTE*	*THE REASON*
Genesis 22	Isaac, Abraham's "only son" Gen. 22:2	A Ram	"And Abraham named that place The LORD Will Provide, so today it is said: 'It will be provided on the LORD's mountain.'" (Gen. 22:14)
Exodus 12-13 *The Passover*	The Firstborn Sons of Israel	An Unblemished Lamb or Goat	"The blood on the houses where you are staying will be a distinguishing mark for you; when I see the blood, I will pass over you." (Ex. 12:13)
Leviticus 16 *The Day of Atonement*	Israel	Animals, Including a Ram	"Atonement will be made for you on this day to cleanse you, and you will be clean from all your sins before the LORD." (Lev. 16:30)
Revelation 5	Sinners	Jesus, "The Lamb of God" John 1:29	"You [the Lamb] were slaughtered, and you purchased people for God by your blood from every tribe and language and people and nation." (Rev. 5:9)

SESSION VIDEOS

Watch this session's video, and then continue the group discussion using the following guide.

▶ What ideas or phrases stood out to you most in the video? Why?

▶ How do tests reveal the nature and substance of our faith?

▶ Where do you see the gospel foreshadowed in this story?

GROUP DISCUSSION

As a group, read Genesis 22:1-6.

▶ How do you think you would have responded to this call of God if you were Abraham?

⭐ How would you define *faith* based on this test from the Lord?

▶ Where do you see Abraham demonstrating faith in God in these verses?

It's easy to say we trust someone, but the proof of that trust is demonstrated by obedience. We see this truth in this story with Abraham. Here the covenant-making God has tested Abraham's faith by telling him to sacrifice his only son Isaac. This is no small or insignificant request. Abraham not only deeply loved his son, but he also knew that Isaac was the start of God's fulfilling promise to bless all the peoples of the earth through his offspring. God had not only promised Abraham offspring as numerous as the sand, but also that his descendants would restore the world. If Isaac died in this way, then the promise of rescuing the world would die with him. God's test of Abraham went beyond anything we can fathom because its implications affected the salvation of the world.

But in obedient faith, Abraham rose early in the morning, gathered the materials for a sacrifice, and set out for the place God told him to go. After a three-day journey, Abraham saw the place and told his servants to remain with the donkey. He said that he and the boy would go over to the mountain to worship and then return. So he took the wood and gave it to Isaac; he himself carried the fire and the knife, and they set off for the mountain.

Abraham and Isaac headed up the mountain for the sacrifice. Abraham did not know exactly what would happen, but he still trusted in the promises of God.

As a group, read Genesis 22:7-14.

▶ What stands out most to you about Abraham's actions in these verses?

⭐ Why was this such an important demonstration of Abraham's faith?

▶ In what ways do you see a foreshadowing of the death of Jesus in these verses?

At what seemed to be the last moment came a divine interruption (v. 11). The angel of the Lord called out to Abraham and instructed him not to harm Isaac. Mercifully, the test was over. Abraham had proven his faithfulness to God because he was willing to let go of his son, who was most important and valuable to him. If Abraham did not withhold his son from God, he would not hold anything else back from Him either. By not holding anything back from God, Abraham revealed what was truly most valuable to him: God.

God prevented Abraham from sacrificing Isaac, but He did not stop there. Abraham looked up and saw a ram caught in the thicket. So he took the ram and sacrificed it in place of his son, Isaac. Abraham saw the ram as God's gracious provision and substitute for Isaac, evident by what he named the place: "The Lord Will Provide" (v. 14). A sacrifice needed to be made, but God spared the life of the one Abraham loved by providing another to stand in his place.

As a group, read Hebrews 11:17-19.

▶ According to these verses, what did Abraham believe about God?

⭐ Why must we believe the same thing as Christians?

In Hebrews 11:17-19, the New Testament writer gives us inspired insight into this event in Abraham's life. He tells us what Abraham was thinking and what motivated his obedience to the Lord.

Hebrews 11 is considered the "Faith Hall of Fame," and in this passage the author praises Abraham's faith. Faith was the means by which Abraham offered up Isaac when the Lord tested him. Abraham had received a promise that his offspring— his heir—would be the one to bring restoration to the world, and even though God's command to sacrifice Isaac looked contrary to that promise, he showed his willingness to carry it out.

Why did he offer Isaac? Abraham offered Isaac not just because of his faith in God, but because he had faith in resurrection from the dead. He believed God was able to raise Isaac from the grave, just as God had been able to bring life out of Sarah's "dead" womb. (See Gen. 17:15-19; 21:1-5.)

CHRIST CONNECTION

Isaac's question "Where is the lamb for the sacrifice?" echoes through the pages of the Old Testament and is ultimately answered at the beginning of the New Testament when John the Baptist sees Jesus of Nazareth and declares, "Behold the Lamb!"

OUR MISSION

◯ Head

What do you already know about God? How can that knowledge help you trust Him?

What are some things God asks us to do in His Word that may seem counterintuitive? Why does He ask us to do these things?

♥ Heart

Are faith and love more than just an emotion? Explain.

What are some ways we can outwardly demonstrate the internal love we have for God and others?

✋ Hands

When have you sensed God testing you? What did you learn about Him from that experience? What did you learn about yourself?

Like Abraham, we may not know when we are being tested. In what ways should Abraham's story impact our obedience?

PERSONAL STUDY: DAY 1

⭐ **The point: God is faithful to keep His promises.**

▶ **Read Genesis 20:1-18.**

What other time did Abraham lie about Sarah being his sister? What motivated him to do this?

How does this show a lack of faith on Abraham's part?

▶ **Read Genesis 18:13-14.**

Here we see God's messengers telling Abraham and Sarah that they would have a son. How do Abraham's actions in Genesis 20 jeopardize God's promise coming to pass?

Even though Abraham acted carelessly and in unbelief, God remained faithful. What does this say about God's character?

For the second time in his life, Abraham lied about Sarah being his sister, although he tried to justify his deception this time (20:12). Once again, he was motivated by fear as he traveled in a foreign land; he was afraid someone else would kill him because they would want to take Sarah as a wife. Fear, not faith, controlled Abraham in this story. God promised to bless those who blessed Abraham and curse those who treated him with contempt (Gen. 12:3), but Abraham either forgot or disbelieved God's promise in the moment.

But there is another troubling aspect to Abraham's deception. Just before this, God's messengers told Abraham and Sarah that they would have the son they had been waiting on (Gen. 18:13-14). But here, Abraham allowed King Abimelech to take Sarah, presumably to be his wife. Abraham's faithlessness in this moment dishonored his wife and God and jeopardized the promise.

Despite Abraham's failures and mistakes, God intervened and protected and preserved both Sarah and the promise. Abraham's act of faithlessness almost caused much more harm than he could ever have imagined.

▶ **Respond**

How are you struggling to trust God right now? What are some promises of God you need to cling to this week?

PERSONAL STUDY: DAY 2

⭐ **The point: God's grace comes at the perfect time.**

▶ **Read Genesis 21:1-34.**

Verse 2 says that Sarah bore Isaac "at the appointed time." Why do you think it is important that the author notes that this time was appointed? What does that have to say about our own lives?

How old was Abraham when Isaac was born?

What does God say about Isaac and His promise to Abraham in verse 12? Why is this important?

How did God care for Hagar and Ishmael when they were sent away?

God has a way of taking our moments of doubt and our failings and turning them around. When the three men visited with Abraham, Sarah overheard that she would have a son within the year (Gen. 18:10). The couple had waited twenty-five years for this promise. Instead of celebrating and worshiping God, Sarah laughed to herself (Gen. 18:12). When she was confronted for laughing, she denied it out of fear (Gen. 18:15). But within the year, Sarah would find out that nothing is impossible for the Lord (Gen. 18:14).

By Genesis 21, the Lord had fulfilled His promise to Sarah; she became pregnant and had a son at the appointed time (vv. 1-2). The couple named their son Isaac, which means laughter. Sarah declared that God had made her laugh and everyone who heard would laugh with her (v. 6). God truly turned Sarah's skeptical laughter into joyful laughter. Surely every time Sarah called her son to dinner or introduced him to others, she was reminded of how God turned her doubts upside down.

▶ **Respond**

This account reminds us that God's kindness and grace comes to us in His perfect timing. How have you experienced God's kindness and grace when you were doubtful or disobedient?

PERSONAL STUDY: DAY 3

✪ The point: God's tests can refine our faith in Him.

▶ **Read Genesis 22:1-6.**

Go back and read Genesis 21:12. Why does God's command to sacrifice Isaac seem to put God's promise here in jeopardy?

Why do you think God was testing Abraham? How can the testing of our faith be a good thing in the end, though painful in the moment?

Why do you think Abraham was quick to respond to God's command so quickly?

Why do you think Abraham told his servants that after they worshiped, both of them would return?

In the chapters between the previous session and this one, several situations arose in Abraham's life, including a threat to the fulfillment of God's promise when a king named Abimelech attempted to take Sarah as his wife. But God remained faithful, protected Abraham and Sarah, and miraculously provided a son named Isaac (Gen. 21). Isaac was the child of promise; he was the heir through whom the promises would be carried forward.

Some years later, however, Abraham's faith was put to the test. God told Abraham to do something that would horrify any father, but especially the father of the promised son, the first descendant of a family through whom the salvation of the world was to come. This was where the rubber would meet the road for Abraham.

▶ **Respond**

Like Abraham, we may not know when we are being tested. In what ways does Abraham's story impact our obedience?

When was the last time God tested you?

PERSONAL STUDY: DAY 4

⭐ The point: God provides a substitute sacrifice.

▶ **Read Genesis 22:7-14.**

In verse 8, how did Abraham's response show his faith? Explain.

Summarize what took place in verses 9-10.

Do you think waiting until the last possible moment to provide the ram made God any less the provider Abraham and Isaac needed? Why or why not?

What did God's provision of a ram as a substitute teach you about Him?

This picture of sacrifice, of a father's willingness to sacrifice his only son and God's provision of a substitute, is the heart of the Christian faith. Just as God provided a ram as the substitute for Isaac, He provided a Substitute for our sins as well—His only Son, Jesus Christ.

▶ **Respond**

This week, spend some time with a Christian friend, mentor, or parent and discuss the following:
- When has God provided for you in a "last-minute" sort of way?
- What did this reveal to you about your level of confidence and trust in God?

Reflect on how Christ's sacrifice was the ultimate display of God's provision. Thank God for sending His only Son to be a substitute for you.

For further study on God as our provider, read Psalm 34:10; Matthew 7:11; and Philippians 4:19.

PERSONAL STUDY: DAY 5

✪ The point: God calls us to trust His provision.

▶ **Read Hebrews 11:17-19.**

Underline each verb used to describe Abraham. What do these verbs tell you about Abraham's character? His faith?

List each of the actions Abraham took in this passage.

What do those actions tell you about how God wants believers to respond to His call on our lives? Explain.

What did Abraham's actions indicate about his relationship with the Lord?

▶ Respond

From time to time, all of us will experience situations that push us to the limits and test our faith. Abraham modeled a godly response to these situations that all believers can emulate in their own lives.

In what ways are you sometimes tempted to respond to God by clinging tighter to what you love? How can you, instead, learn to offer up all that you are and all that you have to God?

Do you ever have difficulty trusting in God to provide a way for you when the situation seems hopeless? Confess any struggles to God, and ask Him to help you trust in Him no matter what.

For further study about trusting God's provision, read Psalm 9:10 and Proverbs 3:5-6.

GOD WORKS THROUGH A DYSFUNCTIONAL FAMILY

GOD IS MERCIFUL TO USE EVEN THE MOST UN-LIKELY PEOPLE TO BUILD HIS KINGDOM.

INTRODUCTION

Have you ever seen stained glass windows that depict scenes from well-known Bible stories? Stories of Abraham, Moses, Jonah, and the birth of Jesus—all artfully crafted in vibrant colors on panes of glass.

The thing is, however, when you stand very close to these stained glass windows, you can't see the story. Instead, all you see are pieces of jagged glass, bright colors, and indistinct details. Up close it looks like an abstract collage; only when you stand back and take in the entire window can you see the beauty, the intricate planning, and the masterful design that illustrates these events.

God's plan often works this way. Up close in the gritty details of daily life, things look jagged and messed up. There doesn't seem to be cohesion and the particulars don't make much sense. But whenever we look back at our lives, taking in the whole picture, we can see how God has been working all along the way.

 When was a time you thought your life was ruined as a result of something that happened or some bad news? Looking back, how have you seen God work through that difficult situation?

SETTING THE CONTEXT

Years after Abraham and Isaac descended from the mountain where God provided the substitute sacrifice, Sarah died. After that Abraham began the process of finding a wife for his son. In a miraculous display of His providence, God revealed His choice for Isaac. Abraham saw his son marry Rebekah before he himself died. But God's covenant did not die with Abraham. The covenant would now continue through Isaac (see "The Patriarchs," p. 58).

Just as Sarah spent the better part of her life unable to bear a child, neither could Rebekah conceive. But once again God brought life where there was none, and Rebekah conceived twins. Even in their mother's womb, these two boys were at odds. Growing up, their differences could not have been more striking. Esau, the older brother, was the hunter and the favorite of his father, while Jacob stayed closer to home and was his mother's favorite. Most surprising of all, before the twins were even born, the Lord had told Rebekah that the older would serve the younger, turning the customary privilege of the firstborn on its head.

THE PATRIARCHS

Abram/Abraham

Go, and I will give you land, offspring, and blessing. All the peoples on earth will be blessed through you (Gen. 12:1-3).

In faith, Abraham obeyed God's command to sacrifice his son, Isaac, until God provided a substitute (Gen. 22). He is the father of all who believe in God's promises—namely, in Jesus Christ (Rom. 4:11).

Isaac

Stay, and I will be with you; I will give you land, offspring, and blessing. All the nations of the earth will be blessed through you (Gen. 26:2-5).

The son of promise through whom God would carry on His covenant with Abraham (Gen. 17; 21; 26).

Jacob/Israel

I will be with you; I will give you land and offspring. All the peoples on earth will be blessed through you (Gen. 28:13-15).

Born, along with his brother Esau, in answer to Isaac's prayer on behalf of his wife, who was barren. Deceived his father to receive the blessing of the firstborn, which belonged to Esau (Gen. 25; 27). The father of the twelve tribes of Israel.

Judah

The scepter will not depart from the tribe of Judah until He whose right it is comes. The obedience of the peoples belongs to Him (Gen. 49:8-12).

Led his brothers to sell Joseph into slavery out of jealousy and for the profit. Later, he offered himself as a substitute slave to gain the freedom of his brother Benjamin (Gen. 37; 44).

Jospeh

The Lord was with Joseph and sent him to Egypt to preserve life for both his family and the nations (Gen. 39; 45; 50).

Given dreams of authority over his family, which eventually came true in Egypt, though after he was sold into slavery by his brothers and even unjustly imprisoned by his master—evil acts from which God worked out His good plan. Established his family as a remnant in the land of Egypt and provided for their survival and prosperity (Gen. 37–50).

SESSION VIDEOS

Watch this session's video, and then continue the group discussion using the following guide.

▶ What stuck out to you the most from this video about the dysfunctional family of Isaac? Why?

▶ What can we learn about the plan and purposes of God through His work in this family?

GROUP DISCUSSION

No family is perfect. Every family has its challenges. The good news is that God doesn't reserve His love and grace for perfect families. We see this on display in Isaac's family: God can and does use dysfunctional families to carry out His plans.

As a group, read Genesis 27:1-10.

▶ Based on these verses, how would you describe the family dynamics at play here?

▶ Are these verses encouraging or discouraging to you? Why?

★ How should human beings consider their part in God's plan?

One can see the dysfunction of this family in that the parents played favorites. Isaac loved Esau's "manliness" and appreciated his ability to bring back food from the hunt. Rebekah preferred Jacob, so when she overheard Isaac's conversation with Esau, she hatched a plot to help Jacob receive his father's blessing instead of Esau.

The plot was to deceive Isaac into thinking that Jacob was Esau. Jacob would bring goats from their flock so that Rebekah could make a meal that Isaac loved. Jacob protested that even though his father could not see well, if Isaac touched Jacob, then Isaac would realize that he was not Esau. Jacob was concerned that he would be cursed by his father rather than blessed. But Rebekah had everything figured out. She clothed Jacob in Esau's clothes, she put the goats' skin on Jacob to make him hairy, and she prepared a meal her husband would enjoy.

As a group, read Genesis 27:1-10.

After Jacob put their plan into action and lied to his father directly, Isaac ate, drank, and then blessed his son. The aging father gave Jacob a four-part blessing: an abundance of grain and wine, dominion over their family and other nations, and curses for those who curse him and blessings for those who bless him. This echoed God's covenant with Abraham.

▶ When have you been guilty of altering the truth (even just a little) to get something you wanted? How did that work out?

⭐ What do Jacob's actions reveal about the human condition?

▶ How do you see yourself in Jacob?

We are often no different than Jacob. In situations where we find ourselves lying, it is usually because of something we want. (We want others to have a certain opinion of us, so we bend the truth.) Jacob was unworthy. Isaac was unworthy. Abraham was unworthy. And that's the point. We are all unworthy to receive God's blessings and to be used by Him. God's mercy and grace are on display in this passage, not man's worthiness. We cling to that mercy and grace, recognizing our unworthiness before a holy God and God's kindness to pour out His mercy and grace upon us without measure through Christ Jesus.

It might not have been his idea, but Jacob was more than willing to go along with his mother's deceptive plan as long as it benefited him. This is a picture of the human heart, for in our sin we are always prone to choose self-advancement and self-promotion.

As a group, read Genesis 28:10-15.

▶ Why do you think God gave this particular dream to Jacob? What did He want Jacob to know?

⭐ Did Jacob deserve this blessing? Why is that important to know?

In Genesis 28:10-22 we are reminded of God's faithfulness to keep His promises, even to those who are undeserving. After betraying his brother, Jacob fled for his safety. He found a place to stay the night, choosing a stone as his pillow.

The stairway Jacob saw reminds us of the Tower of Babel (Gen. 11:4). The people of Babel had attempted to come before God on their own terms. But this story shows us that if man is to reconnect with God, then it will require God coming down to us. Christianity is different from other religions because we believe God's presence is secured not through our climbing up toward Him but through His gracious descent toward us.

Jacob's stairway gives us a glimpse into the reversal of Babel. The people of Babel were trying to reach God by raising up a tower, and it caused them to be separated all over the planet. But when the offspring of Jacob, God incarnate—Jesus of Nazareth—comes down from heaven, He will be lifted up to draw all people to Himself. He will bless all the peoples of the earth and reunite them in Himself. John 1:51 tells us that Jesus is the true stairway to heaven. He is the One who reconnects earth and heaven.

CHRIST CONNECTION

Jacob's story is a good example of why humanity needs a Savior. Like Jacob, we seek a blessing that is not ours, but we cannot lie, deceive, or trick to receive it. Instead, Jesus shared His blessing with us when He took the judgment we deserve so that we might receive the blessing He deserves.

OUR MISSION

○ Head

In what kinds of situations do we find it easiest to lie? What do those situations tell us about what our hearts crave?

How does God's grace to Jacob encourage us toward repentance?

♥ Heart

Do you find it easy to accept God's grace and mercy toward Jacob in light of his sin?

Like Jacob, in what ways does experiencing the presence of God through Christ transform us?

✋ Hands

What are some common dysfunctions in families? How can God's grace through the gospel overcome these?

What hope does it give you to know God works even through our deceit and sinfulness to accomplish His plan?

PERSONAL STUDY: DAY 1

⭐ **The point: God keeps His promises even when people are unworthy.**

▶ **Read Genesis 26:1-6.**

Underline any words or names that indicate whom God was speaking to in these verses.

What was life like at this time for Isaac and all of Abraham's descendants (v. 1)?

Do you think their predicament seemed to line up with God's promises to them? Why or why not?

Why is it important to know whom God addressed in this passage?

What was Isaac tempted to do about their situation?

What did God instruct Isaac to do? What did God promise to do for him?

Circle the words "because Abraham listened" (v. 5). Why is this significant?

▶ **Respond**

Which of the two following attitudes do you struggle with more: feeling unworthy because of past behavior or feeling worthy because of good behavior? Thank God that the fulfillment of His promises has never depended on your behavior.

✪ The point: God's plan goes forward through a dysfunctional family.

What do you think of when you hear the word *deceit*? Spies? Mystery novels? Betrayal? Usually something negative comes to mind, right? On a sticky note, jot down any thoughts you have about the word *deceit*.

In Old Testament times, both the birthright and the blessing were of vital importance to a family.

▶ Read Genesis 27:1-17.

What was Isaac's initial instruction? Who did he instruct in this way?

List every deceptive act you find in these verses.

What did Jacob and Rebekah's actions reveal about their character? About their relationship with God at that point in their lives?

Families have always been affected by sin and engaged in dysfunctional living. Because of this, family members often blame one another, take what isn't theirs, and so on. No family on earth has ever been or will ever be perfect, but as we saw in today's Scripture, God can still build something great in spite of our imperfections.

▶ Respond

If possible, find out from a parent or grandparent about the faith journey of your family, including the bad and the good. Take notes as you talk, so you can refer to these situations later as an encouragement and testament to God's faithfulness in your own life.

Pray for your family and thank God for including you in His plans, regardless of how you or your family behaved through the years. Ask God to continue to draw each of your family members into a deeper relationship with Him.

For further study on dysfunctional families God used to carry out His plans, read Genesis 3:1-7; 4:8; 2 Samuel 13; and 1 Kings 11:1-4.

PERSONAL STUDY: DAY 3

★ The point: God's plan goes forward through deceitful and despondent sons.

Think of your own sibling or siblings from a TV show or movie. Considering those relationships, how would you define sibling rivalry?

What do you think creates a healthy sibling relationship?

▶ Read Genesis 27:18-40.

Does it seem like it was difficult or easy for Jacob to lie to his dad? Explain.

How did Esau respond when he found out about it?

Imagine yourself in Esau's position. How would you respond to Isaac? How would you treat Jacob?

Do these brothers seem like guys God could use to accomplish His plans? Why might He want that to be the exact reason He would use them?

▶ Respond

God's plan has never been dependent on the faithfulness of people, but that doesn't mean we're excused of all responsibility for our behavior. On a plain piece of paper, list everything in your life you think might stop God from using you for His glory. Now, write the word *Unstoppable* over the list. Thank God that His power doesn't depend on you.

Look back over your list. How can God's grace in the gospel overcome these issues? Journal your thoughts.

For further study on how God brought Jacob and Esau to right relationship with Him and each other, read Genesis 28:10-22; 32:3–33:4.

⭐ The point: God's grace allows us to be involved in His plans.

▶ **Read Genesis 28:1-9.**

Why do you think Isaac finally came around to acknowledging the promise would go through Jacob, not Esau?

What was contained in the blessing Isaac spoke to Jacob? How does this compare to the promise God spoke to Abraham?

Why did Isaac not want Jacob marrying a Canaanite girl? What do we know about the Canaanites from other places in the Bible?

It might be easy to miss the detail of Isaac finally coming around to God's plan of carrying on the promises through Jacob, not Esau. Just before this, Esau was angry and wanted to kill his twin brother. Just after this, we read about Jacob's first encounter with God during his travels. But we can learn a lot from Isaac's blessing here. Yes, Isaac made a mistake in attempting to bless Esau despite God's revealed will for Jacob to be the son of promise. And yes, his family was divided and in strife. But here God demonstrated His patience and grace as He continued to work on Isaac's heart and gave him time to obey. And God is just as patient and gracious with us in our slowness and disobedience.

▶ **Respond**

What disobedience do you need to confess to God today? Repent and thank God for His grace and patience toward you.

PERSONAL STUDY: DAY 5

⭐ The point: God's presence changes us.

▶ Read Genesis 28:10-22.

How do you think this encounter with God changed Jacob?

Is it possible to experience God's presence and not be changed?
Why or why not?

In what ways does sin prohibit us from experiencing the presence of God?

How does God overcome our sin to give us a glimpse of His glory and grace?

Because of His mercy and grace, and for His own glory, God gives us the greatest blessing of all—His presence. Our salvation provides us with many benefits, the foremost of which is being spared from eternal death. But we shouldn't make the mistake of focusing on these benefits and forgetting the greatest blessing of all—God Himself! He will be our God, we will be His people, and we will be together enjoying Him forever. This is at the center of our salvation.

▶ Respond

It is easy for us to focus on Jacob's flaws—he had a number of them, after all. But we can't miss his spiritual sensitivity in this moment. He encountered God and responded appropriately in worship.

How about us? How often have we missed God at work in our lives because we have been too busy, too distracted, or too blinded to Him? May we have the spiritual sensitivity to see God at work in the moment.

How has God been at work in your life recently? How has He grown you, blessed you, and used you?

GOD GIVES JACOB
A NEW NAME

*ENCOUNTERING GOD LEADS TO A FUNDAMENTAL
CHANGE OF IDENTITY AND PURPOSE.*

INTRODUCTION

Many people use the beginning of a new year as an opportunity to get in better shape. They purchase exercise equipment, work out every day, start eating healthy meals, and eventually start to feel better. But like most New Year's resolutions, within a few months people start to slack off and eventually wind up back where they started.

The human heart longs for lasting change, and this longing goes beyond faddish New Year's resolutions. For students, it might be a reputation they want to be free from; for some, it may be a pattern of bad grades. Whatever the case, most of us wonder if transformation is possible.

It's easy to lose hope in change because so often we've tried to make changes only to be disappointed. But at the same time, we are fascinated with transformation stories where this person or that family overcame extreme adversity and how their lives have been changed for the better. It's because of stories like these that we believe change is possible.

 Looking back over your life, what kind of transformations have you seen take place in your family? in the life of a friend? in your own life?

SETTING THE CONTEXT

Jacob had maneuvered his way into receiving both the family birthright and the blessing of his father. But Jacob's choices had left consequences in their wake. His brother, Esau, planned to kill Jacob for his deception. Knowing the danger, Jacob's mother, Rebekah, sent him away to her brother Laban in Haran.

But Jacob had met his match in Laban, for he was a manipulator and deceiver much like himself. Laban tricked Jacob into marrying his older daughter instead of the younger daughter whom Jacob loved. To win her hand too, Jacob had to work another seven years for Laban.

Throughout his time working for Laban, Jacob became very rich and God multiplied his family (see "Jacob's Family" p. 70). The Lord then commanded Jacob to return to the land of his fathers with his large family and estate, but Jacob knew there would be a problem—Esau. With much apprehension, Jacob began the trip home, which led to one night that would define his future.

JACOB'S *FAMILY*

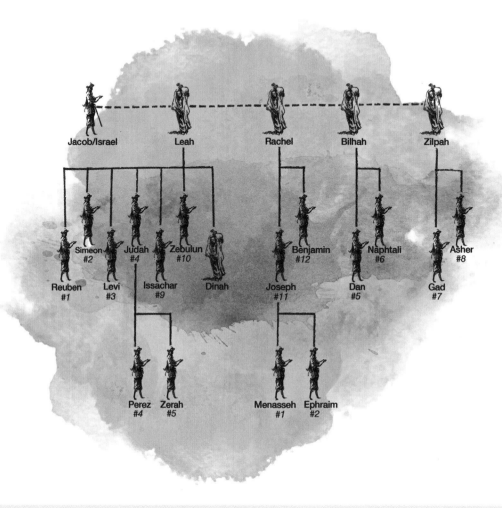

SESSION VIDEO'S

Watch this session's video, and then continue the group discussion using the following guide.

▶ What are some of the ways that this particular encounter with God defined the rest of Jacob's life?

▶ How does the renaming of Jacob remind us of what God has done for us in Christ?

GROUP DISCUSSION

As we will see, Jacob became the namesake for God's chosen people, Israel. Yet the account of Jacob reveals a deeply flawed man. He cheated his brother out of his blessing and lied multiple times to his father.

In the east, Jacob met his future wife Rachel at a well. He loved Rachel and wanted to marry her, so he served her father, Laban, for seven years to win her hand in marriage. But Laban deceived Jacob and tricked him into marrying his oldest daughter, Leah, and Jacob had to work another seven years for Rachel.

Despite Laban's deception, God kept His promises to Jacob. Remember, the promise was land, offspring, and blessing. God gave Jacob financial blessing (though Jacob had schemed to get it), and God blessed him with children. So Jacob had offspring, and he had blessing, but he did not have the land yet.

The Lord told Jacob to return home to the land promised to his fathers, so he journeyed toward Canaan as a rich man with a large family. In order for Jacob to receive the promises of God, however, a transformation needed to take place. Jacob was fearful that his brother, Esau, would seek revenge, so he sent gifts with an envoy ahead of him to soften the blow. As Jacob remained behind, he encountered an unusual man who would change his life forever.

As a group, read Genesis 32:24-27.

Scholars generally agree Jacob's opponent that night was God Himself. While we do not know how this wrestling match began, we do know one of the outcomes of the blow God dealt Jacob. But this blow was not a curse; it was a blessing. Jacob would have to face his physically adept brother—the hunter—and his brother's sizable contingent of men with a physical disadvantage. Self-reliant Jacob would not be able to rely on his own physical ability to fight Esau if it came to that. One touch from God brought Jacob low. And people in a humble posture are the ones through whom God delights in doing great things.

▶ Have you ever felt as though you were wrestling with God? When and why? What happened as a result?

▶ Was God really not able to win this wrestling match? What was His purpose in wrestling with Jacob?

What does this encounter reveal about God?

As a group, read Genesis 32:28-32.

The Lord dealt a second blow to Jacob that night. While this one wasn't physical like the first, in many ways it was more devastating. It came when God asked Jacob for his name. Jacob responded by saying his name out loud. And there it was—the second blow in this match.

Jacob's name has many similar meanings: "trickster," "supplanter," "heel-grabber," and "deceiver." God asked Jacob his name, offering the patriarch the opportunity to confess his character. Jacob did, and then God changed his name. Jacob would from then on be Israel.

▶ List some ways our past mistakes try to haunt and define us.

✪ Why is it significant that God gave Jacob a new name?

▶ What are some ways you have been changed by God through difficult circumstances?

God forced Jacob to own up to his old name and nature. He was a deceiver, but not anymore. Jacob would have the new name of Israel. This new name was symbolic of both the privilege and responsibility of walking with God. Like Jacob, we have been given new names in Christ—we are no longer strangers, enemies, or rebels; we are now God's children.

As a group, read Genesis 35:9-15.

▶ Why do you think God reminded Jacob of his new name?

With the new name of Israel, God was calling Jacob to embrace his identity and purpose as a part of God's plan. When we sin as Christians, it is as if we forget we have been made new in Christ. Fortunately, the Holy Spirit reminds us over and over again that we are the children of God, secure in His hands.

⭐ What are some times we as Christians also need to be reminded of our new identity in Christ?

Notice the progression for Jacob: Blessing (v. 9), New Identity (v. 10), Responsibility (v. 11). In the same way, God blesses us with salvation and transformation so that we can then fulfill His calling on our lives.

What led to the events in this passage? After Jacob returned to his homeland, he reconciled with Esau and blessed him. Later, God commanded Jacob to settle in Bethel and exhorted him to repent of his idolatry. So Jacob got rid of all his family's false gods. In these events, we see the gradual transformation in Jacob's life. Yes, the transformation was slow, but it was progressive. (The same is true with us!)

CHRIST CONNECTION

Jacob's story is a good example of why humanity needs a Savior. Like Jacob, we seek a blessing that is not ours, but we cannot lie, deceive, or trick to receive it. Instead, Jesus shared His blessing with us when He took the judgment we deserve so that we might receive the blessing He deserves.

OUR MISSION

⭕ **Head**

Based upon this account in Jacob's life, what do you think is the significance of a name change?

Does this mean we have to undergo a literal name change? If not, why?

❤ **Heart**

How might God "wrestle" with us in order for us to gain a greater understanding of His grace and love in our lives?

Why is it important that we see these moments as acts of grace on God's part, and not acts of anger?

✋ **Hands**

Whose name do you tend to live under in daily life? Yours or Christ's?

How will we live differently each day by living, first and foremost, under the name Christian?

PERSONAL STUDY: DAY 1

⊗ **The point: God can work through our mistakes.**

▶ **Read Genesis 30:1-43.**

Like Sarah before her, how did Rachel try to take matters into her own hands when it came to her inability to have children?

How did Leah do the same once she saw she wasn't having any additional children?

Even though God never endorsed or approved of having multiple wives, how do we see God use these sinful choices for His good?

What consequences do you think will result within this family because of these sinful choices?

For the third generation in a row, we encounter the theme of barrenness as God forms the nation He had promised Abraham. And once again, as Abraham and Sarah had done, we see people trying to take matters into their own hands. Echoing Sarah's demand for Abraham to have children with her maid, Hagar, Rachel demanded that Jacob have children with her maid, Bilhah. Abraham's grandson had two sons with Bilhah. Then when Leah stopped having children, she gave Jacob her maid, Zilpah, who also bore sons for him.

God used these sinful choices for His good, but they were not without consequences. Rivalry and favoritism would not be confined to Jacob and his four wives. It would spill over onto their children, as with Joseph.

Learning from our sins is important; it is one way we grow in holiness. But it is also important that we learn from the sins of others. Surely Jacob knew the stories of his grandfather. But tragically, he chose to repeat their mistakes.

▶ **Respond**

What lessons have you learned from your failures and how can you encourage others by sharing them?

⭐ The point: God desires we demonstrate integrity in our relationships with others.

▶ **Read Genesis 31:1-55.**

Why did Laban's attitude toward Jacob change?

List all the ways you can think God was blessing Jacob in these verses?

Was Jacob right to leave Laban without telling him? Did this act communicate trust in God?

Why did God want Jacob to return to the land of his father, Isaac?

Jacob traveled to Paddan-aram to find a wife and to flee from his older brother's wrath. Years later, he had that wife—and three others—as well as many children and considerable wealth because of a shrewd arrangement he had made with Laban. Once again, the uncle and nephew found themselves in a match of wits.

It was time for the wayward son to return home; God had told him so (v. 3). And so, as only seemed fitting, Jacob snuck away with his family and possessions, running from Laban without telling him. Of course this didn't go over well with Laban, who chased Jacob and his daughters, catching up to them a week later.

The interaction between Jacob and Laban reminds us that relationships, even within families, can be messy at times. And in order to experience the type of reconciliation the Bible calls for, it is important to remember that both parties bring their individual sin into the relationship. So, we should constantly be asking ourselves, "How has my sin contributed to the situation? How can I try to make things right?" If Jacob or Laban had asked themselves that question, maybe their relationship would have been different.

▶ **Respond**

Are there any relationships in your life that need healing? What steps can you take toward reconciliation this week?

PERSONAL STUDY: DAY 3

⭐ **The point: God's grace gives us a new identity.**

▶ **Read Genesis 32:24-32.**

Describe the struggle Jacob experienced in this passage.

What two things changed about Jacob as a result of the encounter?

What was Jacob's new name? What was the meaning of his name?

▶ **Jacob had another spiritual encounter after he returned from Paddan-aram. Read Genesis 35:9-15.**

Why do you think God reaffirmed Jacob's new identity?

Summarize this encounter in your own words.

What occurred after the blessing in this passage?

▶ **Respond**

Jacob's encounter left him broken and surrendered, which led him to blessing and a fresh identity. What areas in your heart do you need to surrender to God?

Ask God to redeem those broken places and grant you a fresh beginning.

For further study about the Abrahamic Covenant, read Genesis 12:1-3; 15:1-21.

★ The point: God's grace motivates us to action.

▶ **Read Genesis 35:1-8.**

What do you think was going through Jacob's mind when instructed to go back to the place where Esau was?

How did Jacob immediately respond to God's command? Why is this important?

Jacob was in Canaan, but God had something different in mind for the patriarch. So He commanded Jacob to get up and go to Bethel and settle there. Furthermore, he was to build an altar to God where he fled from his brother Esau so many years before.

So Jacob obeyed. But first, he told his family and all of the others with him that they had to do something. They had to get rid of their foreign gods and purify themselves. Everyone gave Jacob their gods and earrings, and he hid them under an oak tree.

Once again, we see Jacob being changed before our eyes. He understood that God was calling him to increased faithfulness—not just in going where God wanted him to go, but also in casting aside other gods from his family's midst. Just as Jacob called on his family to purify themselves and change their clothes, God was doing the same in his life—purifying and changing his heart.

▶ **Respond**

How has God been at work purifying and changing your heart?

Where do you still need Him to work?

PERSONAL STUDY: DAY 5

⭐ **The point: God's grace motivates us toward His mission.**

▶ **Read Genesis 35:9-15.**

What did God reaffirm in these verses?

What was the long-term view of why God would bless Jacob?

Notice the progression of blessing:

Blessing (v.9) ➝ New Identity (v.10) ➝ Responsibility (v.11)

How does this progression echo God's salvation in our own lives?

Everyone wants God's blessing. That's why we pray and ask God for health or for provision or a thousand other things. Asking for blessing is not wrong, of course. It shows how dependent we are on God, and asking Him to bless us is one way of communicating what a good and gracious God He truly is. We ask Him to bless us because we know He delights in blessing His children.

The problem, though, is that many of us do not understand why God blesses His people. We want God to change our lives, but when He does we don't understand why or for what purpose He has changed us. In Scripture, we see that God's purpose in blessing His people is not so they will hoard the blessing for themselves. God blesses His people so they will be a blessing to others, and He changes people so they can be agents of change for others.

We see in Jacob's life that God blessed and changed him so Jacob—Israel—would be the means by which God brought change and blessing to the whole world.

▶ **Respond**

What are some areas in which we ask for the blessing of God without giving thought to how God might want to bless others?

How do God's blessings set us up to serve on mission with Him?

GOD REDEEMS JOSEPH'S ADVERSITY

GOD IS SOVEREIGN AND CAN BRING GOOD OUT OF PAIN AND SUFFERING.

INTRODUCTION

One of the most quoted movies has to be the 1987 film *The Princess Bride* (MGM)—from the battle of wits to the priest saying "marriage"; but most of all, from the line of Inigo Montoya exacting revenge on the six-fingered man: "Hello, my name is Inigo Montoya. You killed my father. Prepare to die!" In the end, he got his revenge!

We all enjoy stories of getting even, don't we? We read books like *The Count of Monte Cristo,* and we sing songs like Taylor Swift's "Mean." We know what it's like to be wronged, bullied, or betrayed in some way.

The reason these stories and songs resonate with us is because we have a deep sense of justice, and when people do wrong, we want them to be held accountable. The problem comes when we want to be the ones who execute justice instead of leaving that role to God. Harboring bitterness or holding a grudge reveals a lack of faith in the justice of God. It reveals that we think we could do His job better than He can. It's also a failure to trust that God can take the evil things done to us and use them as part of His bigger plan for good.

SETTING THE CONTEXT

Jacob spent the night wrestling with God, and he emerged changed with the new name "Israel." And then, to his surprise, Jacob was reconciled with his brother, Esau. Jacob then continued on his way to Shechem in the land of Canaan.

On the way, Israel's beloved wife, Rachel, who was pregnant, began her labor and died during childbirth. Before her death, she delivered one last son for Jacob, Benjamin. Jacob was now the father of twelve sons, and the family took up residence where his father, Isaac, had lived.

Jacob did not learn from his parents' mistake of showing favoritism toward their children, and he loved one son more than all the others. "Joseph's Life" (p. 82) shows when Jacob gave Joseph, the favored son, a beautiful robe of many colors. So not only was Joseph loved more than his brothers, he now wore his father's favor like a garment, and his older brothers longed to rip it off of him.

JOSEPH'S *LIFE*

17 YEARS

In Paddan-aram/Canaan with Family
- Born, the firstborn son of Jacob's favorite wife, Rachel
- Given a robe of many colors by his father, a symbol of his favored status (age 17)
- Given two dreams picturing him ruling over his family (a.17)
- Thrown in a pit by his brothers and sold to Midianite traders (a.17)

13 YEARS

In Slavery/Prison in Egypt
- Sold as a slave to Potiphar in Egypt (a.17)
- Promoted to Potiphar's personal attendant, in charge of the whole household
- Falsely accused of sexual misconduct by Potiphar's wife and imprisoned
- Given authority over everything under the prison warden
- Becomes personal attendant to Pharaoh's cupbearer and baker, also in custody (a.28)
- Interprets dreams of cupbearer and baker, which come true three days later (a.28)

80 YEARS

With Authority in Egypt
- Called before Pharaoh and interprets his two dreams about a coming famine (a.30)
- Elevated to second-in-command over all of Egypt (a.30)
- Oversees collection and sale of grain in preparation for and during famine (a.30-44)

71 Years with Family in Egypt
- Reconciled with brothers; reunited with father and family (a.39)
- Joseph dies; buried in Egypt, but with hope of returning to promised land (a.110)

SESSION VIDEOS

Watch this session's video, and then continue the group discussion using the following guide.

▶ How did God show Himself faithful to His promises throughout the adversity in Joseph's life?

▶ How does the story of Joseph give you confidence to endure hardship and continue on in faith?

GROUP DISCUSSION

As a group, read Genesis 37:5-8,18-20,23-28.

Jacob's favorite son was Joseph because he was born to Jacob's favorite wife, Rachel, in Jacob's old age (Gen. 30:22-24). That's why Jacob made Joseph a robe of many colors, a sign of favoritism toward Joseph and something that caused Joseph's brothers to despise him.

Making matters worse, the story goes on to say (vv. 5-11) that Joseph had dreams about his brothers bowing down to him—not something you want to hear from your younger brother. The text never indicates whether Joseph was right or wrong in recounting these dreams to his family, but it's clear that the dreams were a picture of God's future plan.

⭐ What do you think Joseph was thinking or praying as he was betrayed by his brothers?

▶ How do you see God's work even through this betrayal?

▶ Why do we sometimes envy God's plan for someone else's life rather than accept the one He has laid out for us?

▶ When we try to live out God's plan for someone else, how does that usually turn out?

Despite the suffering that would befall Joseph, God would use the terrible circumstances to exalt Joseph and save his family (along with many others). God gave the family a picture of this plan through Joseph's dreams. It's not surprising that Joseph's brothers did not like the plan, but as we will see, the dreams pointed to the way God would save them from famine and certain death.

We can learn from Joseph's brothers because no matter how much we may dislike what God is doing, we can trust that God's plan for our future is better than any plan we can come up with for ourselves.

What are some dreams you have for your future? How might God's plans be better? Although Joseph was betrayed by his brothers and sold into slavery, God was with him. Joseph became a servant in the house of Potiphar, one of Pharaoh's officers and the captain of the guard. Because God was with Joseph and prospered everything that he did, Potiphar put Joseph in charge of his entire house, and the Lord blessed Potiphar's house greatly. This is one example of how God continued to keep His promise to Abraham that He would bless everyone who blessed Abraham (see Gen. 12:1-3). But just as things were looking up, the situation took a turn for the worst.

As a group, read Genesis 39:19-23.

Joseph was falsely accused by Potiphar's wife, but he did the right thing in rejecting her advances. Despite his innocence, he was thrown into prison. Yet even there, the Lord was with him (v. 21). God had not abandoned him. God showed Joseph great mercy so that even the prison warden put Joseph in charge of all the other prisoners. And once again, the Lord prospered everything that Joseph did.

✪ How do you think Joseph kept from getting bitter during these events?

▶ Can you share some ways you have been reminded of God's presence even during affliction?

▶ What are some challenges you have faced that prepared you to handle future challenges and blessings?

Joseph's life reads like an elevator, with constant ups and downs. He showed his integrity in the house of Potiphar only to be imprisoned. His faith in the continuing promises and work of God was the only way not to become bitter at these twists and turns in life.

As a group, read Genesis 50:15-21.

▶ What does Joseph's response to his brothers reveal about his faith?

▶ Why is it so difficult for us to forgive those who wrong us?

✪ Why is our willingness to forgive others, even when they wrong us, a good indicator of what we believe to be true about the gospel?

You've probably heard the saying "Two wrongs don't make a right." Just because someone mistreats you, it does not give you the right to mistreat them. Repaying evil with evil may be our sinful urge, but it is not the way God works. He is the God who forgives those who sin against Him and who does not repay evil with evil; instead, He overrules evil with good. We are called to follow God by displaying this kind of love to everyone, including our enemies and those who wrong us, because God uses this in His master plan.

Though his brothers clearly wronged him, Joseph acknowledged the continuing ability and willingness of God to take evil and injustice and use it for good. The ultimate example of this is the cross, as God used the evil of Jesus' crucifixion to bring about His master plan of providing salvation from sin and death.

▶ What are some challenges you've faced that you see others facing? In what ways can God bring fruit out of your past affliction by leading you to minister to others in similar circumstances?

CHRIST CONNECTION

God took the evil deeds of Joseph's brothers and used them for His greater plan of providing salvation from the famine. In the same way, God used the evil injustice of those who crucified His Son, Jesus, to bring about His master plan of providing salvation from sin and death.

OUR MISSION

Head

What lessons can we learn from Joseph's victory over temptation?

Why is it important to do the right thing, regardless of the outcome?

Heart

Why do we assume God is there in the good times and gone in the bad?

How does the knowledge that God is with you in hardship help you battle things like discouragement, depression, and isolation?

Hands

How can we show those with whom we disagree love and mercy as an expression of God's love for us?

Since Jesus is the Savior who offers forgiveness to the world, how can we be part of the commission to take the message of forgiveness to all peoples?

PERSONAL STUDY: DAY 1

⭐ **The point: We can trust in God's plan for the future.**

Think about a time you were excited about plans you or your family had for a weekend. How did you respond? Did you want to tell others? If so, how did you tell them?

▶ **Read Genesis 37:3-11.**

How would you describe Joseph's reaction to his dreams? How would you explain his brothers' and father's reactions toward him?

Joseph	His Brothers	Jacob

According to Joseph, what would bow to him? To whom did the "bowing" objects belong?

If his dreams were true, what type of position did this mean he would hold in the future?

Why do you think Joseph's brothers reacted in hostility and Jacob "rebuked him" (v. 10)?

What was different about Jacob's reaction? Why do you think this is important?

▶ **Respond**

What are some of your dreams and desires for the future. How might God's plans be greater than your plans?

Ask yourself: *Have I submitted my dreams to God?* Ask God to begin revealing His plans for you and the small steps you can take to work toward them.

The journey between Joseph's dreams and the fulfillment of God's plan was anything but easy. His journey stretched over the course of years and was filled with pain. Maybe your journey will be similar. How can you build up your trust in God's plan so it guides you through the tough times?

⭐ **The point: Trust in God's process of preparing us for the future.**

▶ **Read Genesis 37:23-28.**

List the actions Josephs' brothers took in verses 23-25.

Imagine you were in Joseph's place. List a few words to describe your reaction to the situation.

Joseph went through a horrible betrayal, but God was not surprised. God is all-knowing of things past, present, and future. Although Joseph would go through a time of suffering, God's plans for him did not change. What does this reveal to you about God's character? His plan for us?

Since God knows and sees all, what should our response be when we face difficult situations?

▶ **Respond**

Is there an area in your life where you find yourself not fully trusting God? Ask God to help you trust Him in every area of life. Share your concern with Him in prayer, trusting He is all-knowing and has everything under control.

Record Jeremiah 29:11 on a note card. Keep it as a reminder to trust God's plan even when you face things you don't understand.

For further study on God's plan amidst difficulties, read Jeremiah 29:11-13.

PERSONAL STUDY: DAY 3

⭐ **The point: We can trust God to use our suffering for His glory and our good.**

▶ **Read Romans 8:28.**

Circle the word "all." How does this verse give confidence to believers when we face difficult situations?

What are some circumstances today's believers might face to make them feel like all things aren't working for their good? Explain.

When have you seen God work a "bad" situation for the ultimate good of one or all of the people involved? Explain.

God uses the tough and unwanted situations we face to build us into vessels that He can use. This prepares us to enjoy the future blessings He has for us.

▶ **Respond**

How has God used a hardship in your past to build your character?

Romans 8:28 is a comforting verse for those experiencing difficulties. Commit to memorizing this verse. Write it out multiple times, save it as the lock screen on your phone, or say it aloud.

Is anyone in your life going through hardship right now? Jot down their names and pray for them this week.

For further study on how trials work for our good, read James 1:2–4.

⭐ **The point: God's faithfulness shows us a picture of forgiveness.**

▶ **Read Genesis 45:7-8.**

Twice in these verses and once more in a previous verse, Joseph made sure his brothers knew it was God who protected Joseph and brought them to this place.

A remnant is a small remaining part of something larger. In other words, when God judged His people, He wouldn't completely wipe them out.

▶ **Read Genesis 45:1-15.**

What was the initial reaction of Joseph's brothers? Why do you think they reacted this way?

Underline all the ways Joseph showed his heart of forgiveness toward his brothers.

Place yourself in Joseph's situation. Would you have so readily forgiven your brothers? Why or why not?

Circle each time Joseph credited God for sending him. Why is this important?

What was the greater purpose for God sending Joseph to suffer in Egypt? Explain.

In what ways does God's faithfulness to Joseph and His faithfulness in preserving all of His people demonstrate how He wants us to forgive one another?

▶ **Respond**

Just as Joseph forgave his brothers, God calls us to forgive. How will this shape the way you approach mistreatment in your daily life?

Joseph expressed tangible behavior that demonstrated his forgiveness. How can you better demonstrate forgiveness toward those who have offended you in your life? List a few ideas.

For further study on mercy and forgiveness, read Matthew 5:43-48.

PERSONAL STUDY: DAY 5

⭐ **The point: God's faithfulness overrules evil with good.**

We've been looking at God's plan and story of forgiveness through Joseph. Joseph's ability to forgive his brothers was remarkable. Why is it so difficult for us to forgive those who have wronged us?

▶ **Read Genesis 50:15-21.**

Why do you think Joseph chose not to repay his brothers with evil?

Do you think you would respond the same way? Why or why not?

What did Joseph do instead?

God used Joseph for a greater purpose. Ultimately, who was influenced by Joseph?

How does this passage demonstrate God's faithfulness and power over evil?

Like with Joseph, there are times God works out challenging situations for His glory. Why do you think it's important to remember God often uses the most difficult situations to shape us into the people He wants us to be?

▶ **Respond**

Joseph's forgiveness was a preview of the ultimate forgiveness that would come through Christ. Christ forgave those who crucified Him and made salvation available to those who believed.

In your journal, draw a line down the middle of the page. Think of some of the negative circumstances in your own life and jot them down in the left column. Now, consider the ways God used each circumstance to further His purpose for you. In the right column, describe how each circumstance helped you grow.

Prayerfully ask God to help you see His will in every challenge you have and will face.

For further study on our forgiveness in Christ, read Philippians 2:5-11.

HOW TO USE THE LEADER GUIDE

Prepare to Lead

The Leader Guide is designed to be cut out along the dotted line so you, the leader, can have this front-and-back page with you as you lead your group through the session.

Watch the session video and *read through the session content* with the Leader Guide cut-out in hand and notice how it supplements each section of the study.

Use the *Session Objective* in the Leader Guide to help focus your preparation and leadership in the group session.

Questions & Answers

★ Questions in the session content with this icon have some sample answers provided in the Leader Guide, if needed, to help you jump-start or steer the conversation.

Setting the Context

This section of the session always has an *infographic* on the opposite page. The Leader Guide provides an activity to help your group members interact with the content communicated through the infographic.

Group Discussion

The Group Discussion contains the main teaching content for each session, providing questions for students to interact with as you move through the biblical passages. Some of these questions will have suggested answers in the Leader Guide.

Our Mission ⬤ ⬤ ⬤

The Our Mission is a summary application section designed to highlight how the biblical passages being studied challenge the way we think, feel, and live today. Some of these questions will have suggested answers in the Leader Guide.

Pray

Conclude each group session with a prayer. A brief sample prayer is provided at the end of each Leader Guide cut-out.

SESSION 1 · LEADER GUIDE

Session Objective

Demonstrate to students that God is the sole creator of the universe, and His creation was good, especially His creation of humanity made in His image, intended to reflect His goodness.

Introducing the Study

Use these answers as needed for the questions highlighted in this section.

⭐ Both science and the Bible point to a definite beginning of the universe. What are some conclusions about God's nature we can draw from His creation of the universe? *We learn that God, who created all things and through which all things exist, is eternal. He has always existed, otherwise He would just be another created being, which is simply not the case. God is the One who created everything we see and know. It is from Him that we understand the meaning of our own lives. It is through Him that all things continue to hold together in our world today. And it is to Him that all glory is properly due.*

Setting the Context

Use the following activity to help group members see the significance of a Christ-centered reading of Scripture.

Ask group members to look at "Seeing Jesus in Genesis" (p. 10) and to come up with a statement that ties together and summarizes these five Old and New Testament connections from the Book of Genesis. (Example: Jesus sets right what humanity destroys through sin, and He does so by sacrificing Himself for the sake of humanity.)

A good summary statement here will lay the foundation for the gospel of Jesus, who died on the cross for the sin of the world. If the basics of the gospel can be found foreshadowed in the first book of the Bible, then imagine how much the rest of Scripture points to the Son, the Word of God, who created all things with the plan and purpose to lay His life down for God's image-bearers.

Group Discussion

Watch this session's video, and then as part of the group discussion, use these answers as needed for the questions highlighted in this section.

✪ What are some of the things we can learn about the nature and character of God from these verses alone? *God is eternal and exists outside of time. God is all-powerful, the Creator of all things. God is good.*

✪ Why does God call each step of His creation good?

> Is it morally good? How so? *Yes. When God created everything, there was no sin in it.*
> Is it aesthetically good? How so? *Yes. You don't have to stare at the Grand Canyon or a sunset for long to realize that the work of creation is beautiful.*
> Is it usable? How so? *Yes. When God created something and called it good, He was saying it was doing well at performing its intended purpose and design.*

✪ Why is it important that we recognize that all humans are created in God's image? *Being created in the image of our Creator means humanity is fundamentally distinct from the rest of creation. It means all humans are created with inherent value, worth, and dignity as a result of bearing God's image. Seeing people as created in the image of God, just as we are, can also help us spot injustice in the world and work toward justice for the oppressed. Treating people with respect as image-bearers of God honors the God who made all human beings.*

✪ How does it change our overall perspective to recognize that all things were created by the Son and for the Son? *We can no longer take things for granted nor live for our own selfish pursuits and desires. Everything we see and interact with and use in creation should serve the purpose of honoring the Son of God. People who live only to please themselves are missing their true purpose in life, and we who know Christ can share His gospel with them.*

Our Mission

◯ How does knowledge of God's sovereignty over all creation influence the way you think about your circumstances? *It should help us recognize that no matter our circumstances, however painful or lonely they may be, God is both good and ultimately in control. We can trust Him and in His timing to work through whatever difficult circumstances we face to make us more like His Son each day.*

Pray

Close your group in prayer, thanking God for His creative power and praying for a greater vision to live out what it means to bear His image.

SESSION 2 · LEADER GUIDE

Session Objective

Show how deep and widespread sin is by surveying the rapid descent in Genesis 3–11. The main takeaway should be how terrible our sin is and how God is right to judge us for it, but still we see God's hope and grace all along the way.

Introducing the Study

Use this option as an introduction to talk about the nature of sin, uncovering how your students currently think about sin—whether sin can be reduced to wrong actions and/or thoughts, or whether it stems from something deeper, a heart rebellion against the goodness of God.

Setting the Context

Use the following activity to help group members see the grace of God in providing salvation for sinners who likewise deserve judgment along with the wicked.

> On a scale of 1 to 10 (1 being carefree; 10 being holy wrath), ask group members to plot their own sense of justice and judgment when they have been wronged and sinned against by someone else. Then ask group members to look at "Salvation Through Judgment" (p. 22) and to reflect specifically on the means of God's judgment (a "10") in comparison with our own sense of judgment. Then encourage them to see God's amazing grace in the salvation column to save sinners who deserve His judgment.

Read this paragraph to transition to the next part of the study:

While the theme of sinfulness is pervasive in Genesis 3–11, so also is the refrain of God's love and grace. Keep an eye out for the signs of God's "salvation through judgment" as we continue our discussion.

Group Discussion

Watch this session's video, and then as part of the group discussion, use these answers as needed for the questions highlighted in this section.

 What can we learn about our own sin from the serpent's temptation and Adam and Eve's response? *1) Acts of sin in our own lives show a distrust of God and His Word. 2) Sin is appealing to our eyes and our desires, and we can easily*

rationalize our choices to give in to sin. 3) Sin always results in shame and broken relationships.

⭐ The Bible tells us that God grieved before His judgment took place. What does this tell us about His character and how He views sin in our lives? *The fact that God is grieved over sin tells us that He is a loving Father who will not simply overlook or turn His head to the pain and disobedience of His children's sin.*

⭐ How did the people's work demonstrate a prideful disobedience? *Pride is at the root of their rebellion for the simple reason that pride rejects the wisdom and authority of God our Creator. Pride manifests itself by choosing to go my own way instead of God's way, essentially making myself the god of my life.*

Our Mission

⊙ How might a right perspective on sin help us have a right understanding of God's grace? *When our eyes are opened to the reality of sin—to its pride and rebellion against a good God, and the consequences that it unleashes to those around us—we begin to see God's love and grace in a whole new light. God wasn't obligated to show grace and mercy or even provide a way to be made right before Him again, but He did, making His love all the more overwhelming in our hearts.*

✓ What happens when you only focus only on the behavioral aspect of sin and not on what is taking place within the heart? *The heart, representing the center or essence of a person, is what directs that person's behavior. It is the command center. Thus, if one has a covetous heart, that may result in the physical act of stealing. The heart is the root, where the behavior is the fruit of one's life. If we were to only focus on the behavioral aspect of our sin, we would never actually confront the root issue that causes us to do what we do. To use an analogy, if we see a polluted river, it is one thing to deal with the pollution as it flows downstream. That's not necessarily a bad thing, but its not the most important thing. The best thing is to travel upstream to the source of the pollution, which in this case, is the human heart. Only by dealing with sin at the heart level can we effectively deal with it at the behavioral level.*

Pray

Close your group in prayer, asking God for wisdom to identify sin for what it truly is and to help others do the same so we can find grace and forgiveness in Jesus.

Session Objective

Show how God formed a new people through Abraham and how God would use this people to bring the answer for sin—Jesus, who provides salvation for all who have faith in Him.

Introducing the Study

Use this section as an opportunity to talk about the nature of relationships and the difference that exists between relationships viewed as a covenant and relationships viewed as a contract.

Setting the Context

Use the following activity to help group members grasp the reality and implications of faith in God to fulfill His promises.

On "Abram's Journey" (p. 34), point out Ur at the starting point of Abram's migration and note the location of Babylon on the route to Haran and then Canaan, the promised land. Ask someone to estimate the distance traveled from Ur to Canaan (about 1,200 miles), and then ask the group how far such a distance would take them from your present location. Invite them to imagine leaving their home and extended family to move there based solely on the promises of God. Then ask the following questions: What challenges and difficulties might you encounter? What would faith in God's promises require of you?

Read this paragraph to transition to the next part of the study:

Abram obeyed God's call to leave his home and family and travel to an unknown land, all in faith that God would do what He said He would do. Abram had his share of doubt and missteps on his journey, but God kept showing up, and Abram believed.

Group Discussion

Watch this session's video, and then as part of the group discussion, use these answers as needed for the questions highlighted in this section.

⭐ What does Abram's response reveal about his faith and about the nature of faith in general? *1) By necessity, faith leads to obedience. 2) Faith is not based on evidence of a promise's fulfillment but based on the goodness and reliability of* the One who makes the promise. 3) Faith in God will lead to choices that defy the expectations of the world.

⭐ What are some ways that we, like Abram, try to take matters into our own hands? *1) We might copy homework from a friend instead of doing the hard work ourselves in order to achieve the grade we desire. 2) We can act on our own without prayer or wisdom from God's Word and from God's people. 3) We might seek vengeance against someone who has offended us, even though God says vengeance is His to repay (Rom. 12:19).*

⭐ In what ways does God call Christians to be set apart today? *1) God calls Christians to love others unconditionally, regardless of family, culture, socio-economic status, or race. 2) Christians should live holy lives reflecting the goodness of God and His wisdom for relating to others and creation. 3) Christians are called to live for the mission of God and His glory rather than for their own personal kingdoms on this earth.*

Our Mission

⬤ God uses flawed and imperfect people in His good work in the world. What are some ways this encourages us? *The story of Abram (Abraham) and the other patriarchs who followed him reminds us of God's unending faithfulness, grace, and mercy. God did not invite the morally excellent into a covenant relationship—He invited the immoral. He didn't invite the expected, but the unexpected. Then God transformed their identities and their lives into shining examples of faith. Abraham, Isaac, Jacob, and Joseph all had significant flaws, yet each one is recorded in the "Faith Hall of Fame" in Hebrews 11. Not because of who they were or what they did, but because of who God made them and what He did through them.*

Pray

Close your group in prayer, asking God to help you and your group live holy lives amongst the peoples and nations of the world, set apart for the glory of God in Christ.

SESSION 4 · LEADER GUIDE

Session Objective

Show how God tested Abraham to reveal his faith in God's promise to bring salvation to the world through his family, and also explain the types of "Jesus" we see in Isaac on the altar and the substitute ram.

Introducing the Study

Use this option to have a conversation with your students about personal loss and how we, as humans, may respond to loss in different ways. As Christians our reaction to loss and pain should be fundamentally different due to our beliefs about Who God is, and what He is doing in our lives.

Setting the Context

Use the following activity to help group members see how the Lord provides both preparation for tests and help in the midst of tests.

Instruct group members to look at the first row on "The Lord Will Provide" (p. 46). Then ask the following questions:

"How does the phrase 'only son' recall God's preparation of Abraham leading up to the test He was about to give him?" *God had promised a son to Abraham and Sarah, and though they had taken matters into their own hands on more than one occasion, the Lord preserved them and His promise. And He fulfilled His promise through a miracle in their old age. The Lord had been faithful to His word, and He wouldn't change that with this test.*

"How do the next three rows relate to the first?" *The Israelites were the people descended from Abraham through Isaac. The Lord provided atonement for their sins through sacrifices. But Jesus, Abraham's promised "seed," was the ultimate sacrifice for sin, and in Him is the blessing to all peoples that the Lord promised through Abraham.*

Group Discussion

Watch this session's video, and then as part of the group discussion, use these answers as needed for the questions highlighted in this section.

 How would you define faith based on this test from the Lord? *1) Believing God*

is good and faithful even when circumstances challenge that belief. 2) Faith means laying down everything we want or have in order to obey God. 3) Believing God can do the impossible and that He will keep His word.

⭐ Why was this such an important demonstration of Abraham's faith? *1) Abraham had received in his old age a son to carry on his legacy, and here he was willing to sacrifice his son because God had told him to. 2) Abraham trusted God completely for the well-being of himself, his son, and the entire world. 3) Abraham's willingness to obey gave evidence of his faith in God and set the example of faith in God/Jesus for all who would come after him.*

⭐ Why must we believe the same thing as Christians? *1) Christians must believe in the resurrection of Jesus or else we are without hope and remain dead in our sins. 2) Christians believe that God has a blessing for the entire world in Jesus, so we must tell about how the Lord has provided Jesus for our salvation from sin. 3) We can faithfully share the gospel without fear of consequences because we believe and know that God has the power to raise the dead.*

Our Mission

⭕ What are some things God asks us to do in His Word that may seem counterintuitive? **Why does He ask us to do these things?** *God frequently asks people to do what may seem counter intuitive. We are instructed to love our enemies (Matt. 5:44); to lay our lives down if we want to save them (Matt. 16:25); to deny ourselves and take up our crosses (Matt. 16:24), and so on. Other examples could be included, highlighting the fact that what may not seem to make much sense from a human perspective is actually divine wisdom at work.*

▼ Are faith and love more than just an emotion? Explain. *Faith and love is only a theory until it is demonstrated. And when we do demonstrate faith and love, we provide it with real weightiness—to the one we love and to ourselves. God used this test to validate Abraham's faith and prove the authenticity of his love. It was not pleasant or easy for Abraham—tests never are—but in the end it was for Abraham's good and God's glory.*

Pray

Close your group in prayer, asking God to help you and your group live as those who are confident in the resurrection from the dead.

SESSION 5 · LEADER GUIDE

Session Objective

Show how God used a dysfunctional family plagued with sin and strife to bring about His purposes, revealing that the success of God's plan is not based on our merit but on His power, mercy, and grace.

Introducing the Study

After going through the intro option and discussing how God can work through difficult situations and use them for His good purposes, read this sentence to transition to the next part of the study:

Sin could not stop God's plan; rather, God advanced His plan to deal with the sin of the world not by working around sinful humanity but through them.

Setting the Context

Use the following activity to help group members see the depth of God's power, mercy, and grace.

> Call attention to "The Patriarchs" (p. 58), and recount the following facts about the patriarchs. Abraham: Believed God's promises; twice lied about Sarah being his sister; tried to build his family through Sarah's servant; laughed at the thought of God giving a son to him and Sarah in their old age. Isaac: Prayed for Rebekah to have children; lied about Rebekah being his sister; showed favoritism between his sons; ignored God's word about the older serving the younger. Jacob: Lied and deceived his family members; showed favoritism between his sons; believed God's promises.

Ask: "At what point would you have given up on this family and started over?"
Then state: "God's ways are higher than our ways (Isa. 55:8-9); our salvation is proof of that."

Group Discussion

Watch this session's video, and then as part of the group discussion, use these answers as needed for the questions highlighted in this section.

⭐ How should human beings consider their part in God's plan? *1) We are to submit in faith to God's plan and purpose for the world and everything in it. 2) We*

should obey the revealed will of God in Scripture—love God and love others. 3)
We should not take matters into our own hands for our own purposes.

⭐ What do Jacob's actions reveal about the human condition? *1) Human beings are*
by nature selfish and self-centered. 2) We fear consequences but can easily
justify our actions to gain what we want. 3) We are prone to use anyone, even
the people we love, to fulfill our desires.

⭐ Did Jacob deserve this blessing? Why is that important to know? *1) No, Jacob*
did not deserve God's blessing. This reveals God's great faithfulness to His
promises—He will do what He said He will do. 2) God is a God of grace and
mercy, and He will never cast out His children. 3) Relationship with God is
ultimately not a matter of what we do but what He has done.

Our Mission

◯ How does God's grace to Jacob encourage us toward repentance? *Like Jacob,*
we have messed up. We have also lied and deceived. But the response of grace
and the offer of repentance that was given to him is offered to us as well. God is
good and gracious. He is still willing to offer forgiveness and restoration and the
opportunity to be used by Him in extraordinary ways.

🅥 Do you find it easy to accept God's grace and mercy toward Jacob in light of his
sin? *It is difficult to read the story of Jacob and fail to see the depth of love that*
God has for him. His unworthiness casts a darkness over his life that serves to
make God's mercy and grace to him that much brighter. And it is here that we
have a choice to make. We can read about Jacob and walk away in frustration.
Why does he deserve such love? Why does he deserve such graciousness and
kindness? Or we can read about Jacob and drop to our knees in awe instead.
We have also failed to live up to the goodness that God intends for us, and yet
God has been merciful.

Pray

Close your group in prayer, thanking God that His blessing of the gospel is not
dependent on our goodness but on His grace.

Session Objective

Show that even while God can work through His people no matter what, in His kindness, God works in us to change us for our good and His glory.

Introducing the Study

Use this option to discuss what real transformation looks like in the life of a person.

Setting the Context

Use the following activity to help group members see God's plan of redemption at work.

Ask group members to number the sons of Jacob (answer: twelve). Point out that God changes Jacob's name to "Israel," so the children of Jacob become the twelve tribes of Israel, but still not in the way we would expect.

Levi: The Levites become the tribe of priests and are not considered one of the twelve tribes of Israel because they belong to the Lord.

Joseph: This son is favored by Jacob, being the first son of his beloved wife Rachel. He himself is not considered one of the twelve tribes but instead gets a double portion of Jacob's inheritance because his two sons are taken by Jacob and blessed as sons equal with their uncles.

Judah: The promised line of kings that God had declared would come through Abraham, Isaac, and Jacob comes not through Jacob's firstborn son, Reuben, nor through his favored son, Joseph, but through his fourth son. And the promise is carried on through Perez on account of more sinful activity in Genesis 38. Judah is front and center in the struggles in Joseph's life, but God works in him to change him, just as He works in Jacob's life.

Group Discussion

Watch this session's video, and then as part of the group discussion, use these answers as needed for the questions highlighted in this section.

⭐ What does this encounter reveal about God? *1) God is merciful toward His children. 2) God is gentle and patient with His children. 3) God asks questions with a purpose.*

⭐ Why is it significant that God gave Jacob a new name? *1) Jacob's old name described who he was—a deceiver. 2) God changes people so they become who God wants them to be. 3) Jacob's character needed work, and God accomplishes that work Himself.*

⭐ What are some times we as Christians also need to be reminded of our new identity in Christ? *1) When we are tempted to sin. 2) When we have sinned. 3) When we struggle with doubts and depression in the midst of our circumstances.*

Our Mission

⭕ Based upon this account in Jacob's life, what do you think is the significance of a name change? *Some people can relate to Jacob's name change because they too have chosen new names after trusting in Christ. For example, some Muslims will take on Christian names to replace their Islamic-origin names, such as changing Muhammad to David or John. However, there is something much more important than a changed name: a changed identity. When we trust in the Lord for our redemption, we take on new identity as followers of Christ, the One who fights for us. From that moment on, neither the patterns of this world nor our own selfish desires and interests run our lives. We are no longer traveling a path that leads to death and destruction. Rather, our new identity reflects that we belong to the Giver of life.*

🔻 How might God "wrestle" with us in order for us to gain a greater understanding of His grace and love in our lives? *While we shouldn't reduce Jacob's wrestling with God to a one-to-one with our own struggling with God, we can certainly see parallels. God will wrestle with us too for the same purpose—to mold us and shape us in His image so we can be His redemptive force in the world. For some of us, it will take a decisive (wrestling-match) "blow to the hip" to shake us out of our worldly habits and patterns. For others, the Lord may use less physical and more emotional means to wake us up from our earthly slumber. We may experience drawn-out times of perceived spiritual drought or emotional duress. Whatever it takes, God will grapple with us to move us from where we are to where we need to be. This act of love and kindness may be challenging in the darkness of the night, but the morning's light reveals its beauty.*

Pray

Close your group in prayer, asking God to remind you this week of your new name in Christ.

Session Objective

Show how God will bring about His plan not only through sinful people, as we saw with Jacob's family, but also through sinful situations—nothing will prevent the fulfillment of His promise.

Introducing the Study

Use this section to introduce the belief that God can use difficult and even tragic circumstances for our good and His glory.

Setting the Context

Use the following activity to help group members see how the life of Joseph points forward to the life, death, and resurrection of Jesus.

Ask group members to look over the summary of "Joseph's Life" (p. 82) and to note connections and parallels with Jesus' life, death, and resurrection. The pattern of Joseph's life is one of favor, humiliation, and then exaltation, just like the pattern of Jesus' preexistence, incarnation, crucifixion, resurrection, and ascension. Furthermore, Jesus is betrayed, oppressed, falsely accused, and lifted up to be the blessing to the world, in which He reconciles people from every tribe, tongue, and nation together as one family of God through faith in Him.

Group Discussion

Watch this session's video, and then as part of the group discussion, use these answers as needed for the questions highlighted in this section.

⭐ What do you think Joseph was thinking or praying as he was betrayed by his brothers? *1) He could have been thinking about justice, revenge, and vengeance. 2) He might have prayed to God with questions and doubts because his circumstances were nothing like his dreams. 3) He likely prayed to be rescued and returned to his father and family.*

⭐ How do you think Joseph kept from getting bitter during these events? *1) He recognized that the Lord was with him and hadn't forsaken him. 2) He continued on with what he knew to do: obey the Lord and be a blessing to others. 3) He looked for the blessings of God even in the midst of his unjust suffering and hardship.*

✪ Why is our willingness to forgive others, even when they wrong us, a good indicator of what we believe to be true about the gospel? *1) When we recognize the depth of God's mercy and grace to forgive us as unworthy sinners, we can have a heart filled with God's grace and mercy to forgive others. 2) The gospel says that no one is beyond the reach of God's forgiveness, so we shouldn't withhold our forgiveness either, as if we were higher than God. 3) Jesus came into the world to save sinners, and He forgave the sinners who crucified Him; we can do no less than forgive as our Savior did.*

Our Mission

◯ What lessons can we learn from Joseph's victory over temptation? *Joseph's story challenges our thinking about our integrity and our actions. Joseph did what was right and fled from the sexual temptation of Potiphar's wife, yet was still sent to prison. Even though he suffered for doing the right thing, he maintained his integrity and would be used by God in the long run to save many nations.*

✋ How can we show those with whom we disagree love and mercy as an expression of God's love for us? *Christ died on the cross in order to fully forgive all of our sins, and His forgiveness is the fuel to forgiving those who sin against us. Refusing to forgive is not just disobedience; it's unbelief. Holding a grudge against someone reveals that we believe the cross of Christ is enough to forgive our sins against God, but it is not enough to forgive the sins committed against us.*

Pray

Close your group in prayer, praying specifically for those in your group to remain faithful during seasons of adversity.

Get the most from your study.

Customize your Bible study time with a guided experience and additional resources.

From cover to cover, the Bible is the story of God's plan to redeem sinners through Jesus. It is the story of the gospel, and Gospel Foundations tells that story. In Volume 1, *The God Who Creates*, you will witness the opening scenes of God's story, of how He laid the foundation of the earth with the power of His Word, and how He begins to unfold His plan to redeem humanity by first establishing a covenant with Abraham. It is a story of rebellion and redemption, of sin and salvation, of failings and faith. Here is a book that shows us who we are in our sin and who God is in His grace.

This Bible study will:

- Help students understand the chronology of key figures and events contained in the book of Genesis.

- Trace the gospel thread throughout Genesis, showcasing God's unfolding plan to redeem humanity through Jesus.

- Show students how the accounts in Genesis are capable of transforming the way we think, feel, and live today.

Lifeway designs trustworthy experiences that fuel ministry. Today, the ministries of Lifeway reach more than 160 countries around the globe. For specific information on Lifeway Students, visit lifeway.com/students.

ADDITIONAL RESOURCES

GOSPEL FOUNDATIONS: VOL. 1, LEADER KIT
Teaching videos and additional materials for a six-session study on the Book of Genesis
Leader Kit: (9781535915717)
Digital Leader Kit: (9781535915779)

GOSPEL FOUNDATIONS: VOL. 2-6
Continue the series with volumes 2-6, including optional leader kits with videos and additional materials available

GOSPEL FOUNDATIONS FOR ADULTS: VOL. 1
A six-session Bible study for adults on the Book of Genesis
Book: (9781535903585)

E-book and video sessions available at www.lifeway.com/gospelfoundations